NAVAL HERITAGE

Gregory Clark

ROYAL NAVAL MUSEUM, PORTSMOUTH

LONDON HER MAJESTY'S STATIONERY OFFICE

First published 1981

ACKNOWLEDGMENTS

Thanks are due to the following Service Museums for permission to reproduce illustrations and photographs in this book:
The Royal Naval Museum, Portsmouth
The Royal Marines Museum, Eastney, Portsmouth
and The Submarine Museum, HMS Dolphin, Gosport.

Designed by HMSO Graphic Design

ISBN 0 11 290346 0 (limp cover)
ISBN 0 11 290365 7 (cased)

Foreword

by Admiral Sir James Eberle G.C.B.
Commander-in-Chief, Fleet, Allied Commander in Chief Channel, Commander in Chief Eastern Atlantic

Britain, as an island nation, has always been dependant upon the sea. The sea is the main highway to and from these islands, for trade and for people and for much of the food we need; and the British have earned a reputation second to none for their use of the sea and its resources. The sea, with its opportunities and limitations, is a continuous theme throughout British history and our naval heritage marches hand in hand with the story of our nation. The Royal Navy has always existed to safeguard 'such as pass on the seas upon their lawful occasions' (as the Naval Prayer puts it) and to protect both our British shipping and our wider National interests both at home and overseas.

For the past thirty years, the United Kingdom has been a member of the greatest and most successful Alliance for the safeguarding of peace and freedom which the world has ever known – the North Atlantic Treaty Organisation. As its name implies, this Alliance has the sea at its core, and the Royal Navy, in co-operation with the other Navies of the Alliance, plays a vital role in NATO's strategy for deterring war and for defending the national security interests of its member Countries.

As well as being the NATO Commander-in-Chief for the waters surrounding our land, I am responsible as Commander-in-Chief of the British Fleet, for the efficient operation of Her Majesty's ships world-wide. These responsibilities involve me in frequent dealings with the Navies of other countries, for which the background of a wide knowledge of our own maritime heritage and the history of the Royal Navy provides a most useful perspective; as, indeed, it does for anyone concerned or interested in the nation's development and its future.

The author of this book is a naval officer, now retired, who is Curator of the Royal Naval Museum. Much of his experience is reflected in these pages which present a balanced account of the Royal Navy's history, with a special accent on the two World Wars, the types of warships in service today and the men and women in it. This book has not been written for specialists but I am sure that it will prove a most refreshing appetizer to anyone wishing to learn about Britain's naval heritage.

Preface

'Long as the waves shall roll
Long as Fame guards her Scroll
And men through heart and soul
Thrill to true glory,
Their deed, from age to age,
Shall voice and verse engage;
Swelling the splendid page
Of Britain's Story'

Alfred Austin

In a somewhat different format this book was first published some years ago specifically for the benefit of all Junior entrants to the Royal Navy. The objects were to provide them with some idea of their Naval Heritage and introduce them to the more popular naval customs and expressions. At the request of the publishers, Chapters were also included outlining the types of warships then in service and the various branches that made up the Senior Service.

To give the original publication wider appeal, it has been rewritten and it is hoped it might encourage the reader, particularly those in the younger age group, to learn more of the events mentioned briefly within these pages. Types of warships and naval specialisations alter in sympathy with this ever changing technological world and whilst every effort has been made to ensure accuracy at the time of writing, readers are advised to check from official sources, the information given on these subjects in the relevant chapters.

I am indebted to Admiral Sir James Eberle, GCB, Commander in Chief Fleet, for his kindness in writing the Foreword to this book and to the Directors of the Royal Naval Museum, the Submarine Museum and the Royal Marines Museum who have allowed me to use some of their photographic illustrations.

January 1981 G.C.

CONTENTS

PART ONE

PART TWO

PART ONE

CHAPTER ONE

The Beginnings of the Royal Navy

The beginnings of the Royal Navy go back to the time of Alfred the Great, that great Anglo-Saxon king who in his reign of almost thirty years united his people and kept order on land as well as on sea. This was necessary because new enemies – the Vikings from Denmark, Norway and Sweden – often tried to invade the country. When Alfred died, the Danish Vikings, with their long boats (sometimes propelled by as many as sixty oars, as well as the one huge sail so typical of Viking boats), were successful in invading England. Later still the Normans, who joined their military skill to sea-power, also conquered the English. In the end, the union of these three peoples, Anglo-Saxons, Vikings and Normans, made the love of the sea even stronger in the English nation than it had been before.

The nearest resemblance to the Royal Navy in medieval times was the duty imposed on the Cinque Ports to provide ships for the defence of the south-east coast. In the reign of Edward I some of these ships, while taking on water in Normandy, were attacked by French fishermen and one English sailor was killed. In an attempt to take revenge, the Cinque Ports mariners were defeated by the French, who hanged their prisoners – with a dead dog hung alongside each one to show their contempt for Englishmen.

It was not until the reign of Edward III that the English sailors had their full revenge, when in 1340, at the battle of Sluys in Flanders, the French fleet was destroyed. Edward collected over 200 ships for this battle, and when they met the French in the harbour of Sluys the combined fleets looked like a forest because of the vast number of masts so close together. In the very close action that followed flights of arrows darkened the skies, huge stones and missiles of every kind fell in all directions; and, when the crews boarded each other's ships in mortal combat, the sun was reflected from their lances and swords as they dealt out destruction and death. The French were defeated with terrific slaughter in this action, which showed the prowess of Englishmen as fighters and seamen.

The search for trade routes

When Henry VII came to the throne the main export of this country was wool, which found a market in the Low Countries, at the mouth of the River Rhine. The more profitable trade in the northern seas of

Europe was in the hands of the German merchants of Hansa, whilst in the south the sea trade was carried on by the great maritime republic of Venice. From as early as the 5th century Venice was the great market and centre for goods from the East, and Venetian traders occasionally came to England to sell the wonderful silks and spices of the Orient. Quite naturally, there was a demand in England for such goods, and Henry VII was the first king since Alfred's time to realize what wonderful trading opportunities lay ahead for English seamen. The current belief that the Earth was flat and consisted of only three continents, Europe, Africa and Asia, was put in doubt by the ideas of a German, Martin Behaim. He drew these three continents on a globe, thus suggesting that the Earth might be round. This indeed was something new, and Behaim's globe fired the imagination of all seamen, in particular as it opened up the possibility of a sea route to Asia and the mysterious East.

Besides the valuable carpets, silks and spices that were brought overland to Europe from the East, came the travellers' tales of these mysterious lands and peoples. As a boy, Christopher Columbus had heard such tales from travellers such as Marco Polo, and in 1492, assisted with money and ships by Queen Isabella of Spain, he decided to test this 'round world' theory. If the world was round, surely another way of reaching the East would be to sail westwards right round the globe? So he sailed to the west, far into the Atlantic, where no European ship had ever sailed before; and although his frightened seamen mutinied, he still sailed on. After five weeks at sea, land was sighted, which Columbus, believing it to be the Indies, named the 'West Indies'; it was, in fact, San Salvador (Watling Island), Bahamas. It is strange to think that this great pioneer never knew that he had discovered the New World, believing to his death that he had found a new trade route to the East.

Henry VII was very interested in the discovery made by Columbus, but he decided to encourage the trade of England with the Low Countries before taking part in voyages of exploration. To help English merchants, heavy duties were imposed on goods imported into or exported from England in foreign vessels, and in addition Henry provided money to build new merchantmen. These new ships were larger than any seen before in England – so large, in fact, that the Royal Dockyard at Southampton was not big enough to carry out repairs to the *Sovereign* and the *Regent*, Henry's largest merchantmen. And so a new dockyard was built – at Portsmouth. As his ships were so large, they could carry greater quantities of cargo, an advantage which was quickly recognised by English traders, who hired them from the king in increasing numbers.

Although these vessels were essentially merchantmen, they were armed as a protection against pirates. By this time the cannon had been produced, a rather clumsy breech-loading weapon which fired a cannon ball weighing about half a pound. These new guns were mounted on the castles, both fore and aft, and on the decks in between; the *Regent* alone carried no fewer than 225 of the new 'toys'. Traders soon found Henry's ships very profitable and many copied their design when building ships for themselves. This was just what the king wanted, for it meant greater trade for England and a large fleet of merchantmen which could be converted to warships if the need arose.

John Cabot

Among the Venetian merchants who came to trade in England during the reign of Henry VII was John Cabot, who believed that by sailing north-west from Europe he would come to the eastern part of Asia, where the spices grew. (Besides the luxury goods of the East, spices were in great demand in Europe for preserving meat.) John Cabot managed to persuade King Henry VII to provide ships and money for an expedition, and in 1497 he set sail from Bristol. A few weeks later, on the other side of the ocean, he came to a rock-bound coast, with dark forests of pine trees covering the hills inland. Although there were signs of habitation, he saw no people and Cabot planted the English flag ashore in the name of the king. It is possible – though not certain – that Cabot was accompanied on this voyage by his son Sebastian, then a boy.

Cabot called the new land, 'New-found Land', but it was very obvious to him that this land was not the rich land of the spiceries, with their densely peopled cities and their teeming markets. So, rather sadly, he returned to England, on the way passing through seas abounding with shoals of codfish. This news he brought back to the fishermen of England, who then began to sail regularly every year to catch the fish off the shores of Newfoundland and bring it back dried or salted to sell in Europe. The ports of the West of England became prosperous on the profits of this trade, and a great impulse was given to the building of sturdy vessels that could withstand the stormy seas of the Atlantic.

The achievements of Spain and Portugal

Two other seafaring nations, Spain and Portugal, had greater success in the search for a trade route to the East. The success of Columbus made the Portuguese very jealous: they had almost found a route to India by sailing round the Cape of Good Hope and hugging the coastline; but this man Columbus had found a short cut to the East, so they thought, by sailing westwards across the Atlantic. And so, to avoid a war between Spain and Portugal, the Pope of the time decided to divide the known world by a line passing through the middle of the Atlantic. Any new route to the Indies found by sailing to the west of that line was to belong to Spain, whilst routes discovered by sailing eastwards were to be Portugal's possession. It was a wise decision, for it prevented conflict between Spain and Portugal and made each country concentrate on one definite route, westwards or eastwards. Very soon the Portuguese were rewarded: in 1497 Vasco de Gama sailed round the Cape of Good Hope and then across the Indian Ocean to India. He returned home with the riches and spices of the East, and Spain, as well as other European countries, looked with envious eyes at Portugal. But Spain kept strictly to the Pope's decision and pressed on with her search for a westward route. Her navigators sailed west, north and south-west; and, after many disappointments, their efforts were successful. Mexico and Peru were discovered, the inhabitants conquered and abundant quantities of gold and silver brought back to Spain. It was obviously not India they had found, for there were no spices in this new land; and, indeed, one of these Spanish navigators, Balbao, who made a landing at Darien (now Panama), climbed a mountain and gazed to the west upon a mighty ocean which was later to be called the Pacific.

Although the Spaniards were delighted with the riches of Mexico and Peru, which soon made Spain the wealthiest country in Europe, they did not forget their original quest – the westward trade route to the East. Eventually, in 1520, Magellan found this route. He sailed on behalf of Spain down the east coast of South America, through the Strait now named after him, and then westwards across the vast Pacific Ocean. He lost his life whilst ashore in the Philippine Islands, but one ship in his expedition returned home to Spain via the Indian Ocean and the Cape of Good Hope. Columbus was right – the world was indeed round, and the East had been found by sailing westwards!

King Henry VIII and the Navy

Meanwhile, in England, Henry VII had been succeeded by his son Henry VIII. The new king was very fond of ships, though he was more interested in building new and more powerful vessels than in taking part in this search for a trade route to the East. He realized that if ever England found herself at war with a European country her island shores must be protected by a navy.

The earliest guns were breech-loaders and were built of wood, strengthened by hoops of iron. The primitive method of breech loading made them exceedingly dangerous, and quite often the explosion killed the gun's crew! During Henry VIII's reign an improved and safer type of cannon was produced – the muzzle-loader. This could fire a shot large enough to hole a warship; but, because of is greater weight and force of recoil, the castles of a ship were not strong enough to support the new weapon. So Henry had the new guns moved to the strongest part of the ship – the cargo deck. Holes or ports were cut in the sides of vessels so that the guns could fire on the broadside. Henry was very proud of this invention, and he caused many new ships to be built, this time not as merchantmen but as warships. His first was popularly nick-named the *Great Harry*. She was a two-decked ship with castles fore and aft, and carried 42 muzzle-loading guns. Most of the new ships were of about 500 tons and carried two or more masts – in fact, the reverse side of the old halfpenny shows a typical ship of Henry VIII's time.

By the end of his reign Henry had built up a fleet of 53 warships and created the post of Lord Admiral (or High Admiral), together with a small Board to advise on naval matters. His reign produced the first ships specially designed for war, and for this reason he has sometimes been called the 'Father of the Royal Navy'.

England renews her search for trade routes

After the failure of Cabot's expedition to find a route to the East, during the reign of Henry VII, it was a long time before England tried again to find trade beyond the oceans. The westward route belonged to Spain and the eastward to Portugal, but many men believed that there was a way to be found to the north-east, so as to sail beyond the regions of snow and ice to the rich kingdom of Cathay; by this they meant northern China, which had been described by the celebrated traveller Marco Polo. About the middle of the 16th century some of the great London merchants took up the idea seriously and provided money to a company called 'the Merchant Adventurers of England for the Discovery of Lands Unknown'. The expedition was led by two English navigators, Sir Hugh Willoughby and Richard Chancellor, with orders to steer to the north-east round the North Cape, at the extreme north of Norway. It was arranged that if they were separated each would wait for the other at the last port in Norway, before sailing on into the unknown seas. Soon after leaving England, in 1553, the ships were parted in a heavy storm and each went on independently but, although Chancellor waited for Willoughby, the latter never appeared and Chancellor had to go on alone. After a while he found himself in a deep gulf, which we now call the White Sea. At last he came across some fishermen who told him that he had come into the country of Muscovy (Russia) and that if he continued his journey overland he would reach Moscow.

Chancellor was disappointed that he had not reached the East, but he continued his journey overland to Moscow, where he exchanged his English cloth for Russian furs and was able to persuade the Czar to grant him the privilege of opening up a trade in furs. It was not until months after Chancellor's return home that it was learned what had happened to Willoughby – he and his crew had been frozen to death in their ship on the Russian coast, where they had been forced to spend the winter after failing to find a passage through the ice. This disaster showed the difficulty of finding a north-east passage to the markets of eastern Asia and caused Englishmen to give up the idea for many years.

CHAPTER TWO

The Elizabethan Age

We all know that Henry VIII made many marriages. When he died, in 1547, he was succeeded by his ten-year-old son Edward. The young king was in poor health and reigned for only six years, being succeeded on his death by his half-sister Mary. Her reign proved also to be of short duration, a mere five years, and of no real naval importance.

Martin Frobisher

But in 1558, after the death of Mary, Elizabeth I – another of Henry VIII's children – ascended the throne. She too, like her father, was very fond of her seamen and immediately gave encouragement to the search for a trade route to the East. Because Chancellor had failed in his search for a north-east passage, an expedition under Martin Frobisher was despatched on a north-west passage beyond the icy coasts of Labrador. Frobisher made three daring voyages in all, but on each occasion he found his way barred by the Arctic ice, and finally returned to England a much disappointed man. For several years the general public was very shy of all schemes of the same kind and only a few of the more far-sighted merchants kept their interest in plans for finding a way to the East.

Hawkins and Drake

Many seamen in the West of England were beginning to seek their profit by preying on the trade of the Spaniards with their new colonies in the West Indies and on the mainland of America. In those days, if one of our sea captains had suffered loss at the hands of the sailors of another nation, he was allowed to take revenge by attacking the ships of that nation. The seamen of Devon were always ready to claim that the Spaniards had robbed their ships. In consequence, all down the western seaboard of Europe there were constant sea fights between our sailors and the Spaniards. One such seaman was John Hawkins, a native of Plymouth. At the beginning of Elizabeth's reign England and Spain were still officially friends, and Hawkins believed he was free to trade with the Spanish colonists in the West Indies, to whom he sold negro slaves brought from the west coast of Africa. The colonists were delighted to get these slaves, but Spain herself frowned on the trade, for really her colonists were not permitted to trade with any but Spanish merchants.

Hawkins became a very wealthy man after his first slave-trading trip, and so he decided to make a second one, this time taking with him his younger cousin, Francis Drake. As before, they traded their cargo of beads, knives and brass wire for slaves on the west coast of Africa, and then set sail for the West Indies. This time the Spaniards were very unwilling to buy the negroes, so Hawkins threatened to compel them to trade by force and even resorted to arms to make them do as he wished. With many of his slaves still unsold, a storm forced him, in 1568, to take shelter in the port of San Juan de Ulloa, on the Mexican coast, a port which was the centre of Spanish power in those seas; and very shortly after Hawkins had anchored there the annual fleet from Spain arrived. At first the Spaniards treated him courteously, but with the arrival of the Spanish fleet they attacked him unexpectedly. Hawkins was greatly outnumbered, and many of the Englishmen were killed or taken prisoner. Among the leaders only Hawkins and Drake managed to escape home to England in the smaller of the English vessels – Hawkins in the *Minion* and Drake in the *Judith*. There was a great cry for revenge, but Queen Elizabeth would not hear of such action, as she knew this would mean war with Spain, an event she wanted to delay until her forces were strong enough.

This forbearance did not please Francis Drake, who decided to take his own revenge against the Spaniards. With two small ships and seventy men he plundered Spanish treasure ships in the West Indies, landed at many places to seize their gold and silver bullion, and returned home in 1573 a wealthy man. The news of his courage and success thrilled everyone and Queen Elizabeth was very proud of her bold captain. In 1577 the Queen gave him permission to lead an English expedition on a voyage round the world; this he accomplished by sailing through the Magellan Strait, then up the western coast of South America, across the Pacific and home through the Indian Ocean and round the Cape of Good Hope. Whilst sailing up the western coast of South America, he attacked and plundered many Spanish ships and returned home with his own vessels laden with gold, silver and precious stones. Francis Drake's name was a terror to every Spaniard, and King Philip of Spain demanded his execution; but Queen Elizabeth, proud of her great sailor, received Drake with honour and knighted him on the deck of his own ship.

The Spanish Armada

When Elizabeth came to the throne, England and Spain were generally on friendly terms, but no Englishman was allowed to enter the Spanish colonies and Philip of Spain was determined to make every country a Catholic one. Since Henry VIII's time England had been a Protestant country, and so also were the Netherlands, ruled over by the King of Spain. When Philip attempted to put down Protestantism in the Netherlands, Elizabeth helped his Dutch subjects with men and money. England and Spain were thus drifting into war, and Englishmen realized that they could defend themselves against the threat of Spain only by their power at sea. Spain claimed to be the mistress of the seas of the New World; and when, in 1580, Philip seized Portugal, the claim to all trade routes both eastwards and westwards was thus held by a single king whose power was a menace to the whole world. War was thus bound to come unless England gave way to the demands of Spain, but Drake's exploits showed that such a step would never be given even a thought. So Philip gave orders for the preparation of a mighty Armada which would carry Spanish soldiers from the Netherlands to invade England. However, rumours of these intentions reached Queen Elizabeth. Drake was sent for and with a squadron of ships he made for the Spanish harbour of Cadiz, where by gunfire he destroyed 10 000 tons of Spanish shipping and thus delayed the Armada for a whole year.

By the summer of 1588 the Spanish Armada, under the command of a soldier, the Duke of Medina Sidonia, was ready to sail; and 30 000 Spanish soldiers, commanded by the Duke of Parma, waited in the Netherlands to be carried in the ships to England. The English fleet was commanded by Lord Howard of Effingham, but it included such expert seamen as Drake, Hawkins and Frobisher. The news that the Armada had been sighted soon spread, and warning beacons blazed all over England. Ships were manned, soldiers mustered and Queen Elizabeth herself rode among her troops at Tilbury, where she remarked, 'I have the body of a weak and feeble woman, but I have the heart of a King, and a King of England too'.

Drake, we are told, was playing a game of bowls on Plymouth Hoe when the Armada was sighted and he stayed to finish the game before he sailed. The English ships were smaller and more manœuvrable than those of the Spaniards, and their tactics were to engage the enemy at a distance and avoid being boarded by their larger opponents whilst their good shooting kept the enemy on the run up-Channel.

Lord Howard, with Drake in company, gave chase to the Spaniards all the way up the Channel, past the Isle of Wight, until the Armada took refuge in the neutral port of Calais. But the English were not to be cheated of victory, and during darkness fire-ships were sent among the Spanish fleet. Although no enemy ship was in fact destroyed by fire, so confused were the Spaniards that they cut their cables and made for the open sea; and after a final engagement next day off Gravelines, a gale blew them northwards. Like bloodhounds, Lord Howard and his gallant seamen tracked their quarry, until they were satisfied that there was no chance of the Armada linking up with the Spanish army in the Netherlands. Many of the galleons were wrecked on the coasts of Scotland and Ireland, and out of the 130 vessels making up the Armada only about 60 ever returned home to Spain. It was the gunnery and seamanship learned in their raids on Spanish colonies that gave Howard, Drake,

Hawkins and Frobisher their crushing victory and made the name of England one to be reckoned with at sea.

Although the defeat of the Armada was a glorious victory for England, it did not mean the end of Spain as a power, and the last years of Queen Elizabeth's reign were devoted to further expeditions against the Spaniards. Our greater freedom at sea led to the beginnings of English colonisation, when in 1590 Sir Walter Raleigh founded what proved to be a promising colony in Virginia from whence he brought back to England potatoes and tobacco.

The last fight of the *Revenge*

In 1591 seven English warships were awaiting the expected arrival of a Spanish treasure fleet in the Azores. As they had been there for many months, the presence of this small squadron became known to the authorities in Spain, who despatched a strong fleet of fifty-three ships under Don Alonso de Bazan to drive off the English ships and escort the treasure fleet home. When this powerful fleet appeared on the scene, the small English squadron could only run for it. Sir Richard Grenville, in the *Revenge*, was delayed however, by having to re-embark a watering party, and by the time he got outside the harbour he found his passage blocked by the Spanish ships to windward. Obstinately refusing, according to some accounts, to 'put his helm up for any Spaniard', he tried to force his way through, but was eventually cornered by several of the larger enemy ships and disabled. The remaining English ships, after a partial action, made good their escape. Early in the action Sir Richard was wounded, but he refused to leave the deck. The fight was carried on throughout the night until the decks of the *Revenge* were covered with dead and wounded; and when morning came Grenville still had no thought of surrender but ordered the gunner to blow up the ship ('Sink me the ship, master gunner, sink her and split her in twain.'). However, the master and others considered that enough had been done for honour and signalled to de Bazan their surrender, stipulating only that they should not become prisoners of war. To this de Bazan agreed. Sir Richard Grenville was carried aboard the Spanish flagship, where he died a few days later. Sir Walter Raleigh wrote an account of the whole event, which is also commemorated by Tennyson's celebrated poem '*The Ballad of the Revenge*', telling the story of the fight of one ship against fifty-three.

CHAPTER THREE

The Dutch Wars

THE DECLINE OF THE NAVY

After the death of Queen Elizabeth in 1603, James I came to the throne. The new king had no interest in the Navy and went out of his way to become friendly with Spain. The wonderful ships that had fought the Armada were left to rot at their moorings, and English seamen, finding themselves without work, offered their services to the Dutch. From being a first-rate sea power at the time of the Armada, England sank to its lowest ebb. Pirates from other countries constantly raided our seaports, laying their hands on anything of value, sometimes even taking away the ships in our harbours. For over twenty years this state of affairs continued, until in 1625 James was succeeded by Charles I, who straight away tried to bring back some of the former glory of English sea power. Charles decided to show Spain that England still had a Navy by planning an attack on Cadiz. Unfortunately, few English seamen could be found, and the only warships available were those that had survived the Armada. So Charles filled these ships with soldiers and sent them off to attack Cadiz. The whole expedition was a failure. Many ships collided with each other on the way and even when the soldiers landed at Cadiz, so bad was their discipline that many got drunk on captured wines. Miraculously they managed to return to Portsmouth, where they were left without food or stores, as everyone was so disgusted with their behaviour.

In 1627 King Charles made a further attempt to show English sea-power, this time by sending some ships to assist the French Huguenots (or Protestants), who were fighting against the French government. The Lord High Admiral, the Duke of Buckingham, was chosen to lead the expedition, but once again there was a shortage of ships and seamen. However, seamen were forced to join what ships there were; and eventually this squadron set sail for the Huguenot stronghold, La Rochelle, in the Bay of Biscay. Once again they were defeated and forced to surrender. Buckingham managed to escape back to Portsmouth; but in 1628, when he asked for volunteers for another expedition, one disgruntled officer stabbled him in the heart.

English sea power was indeed at a very low ebb; pirates still raided our ports and the Dutch openly fished off our coasts and actually landed at will to repair their nets. Charles realised that unless he were to build new ships he would never attract English seamen back to his Navy. And as Charles badly needed money, he reintroduced a 'Ship Money' Bill, by which not only the principal coast towns but also inland counties had to provide money for the Navy. By 1639 twelve new vessels, including the magnicent *Sovereign of the Seas*, had been constructed. It was a beginning, but still nothing in comparison with the size of the Dutch fleet led by Tromp, who proudly boasted that his ships ruled the English Channel. This claim was no idle boast, for the Dutch continued to use English fishing-grounds and merely ridiculed the size of the Ship Money fleet. Parliamentary resistance to the king's attempt to raise money by the 'Ship Money' Bill, and to other unpopular measures, led in 1642 to civil war between the king and his supporters, on the one hand, and the Parliamentary party on the other. After several years of bitter fighting, King Charles was defeated and, falling into the hands of the Parliament was tried and executed in 1649.

The death of the king and the appointment, in 1653, of Oliver Cromwell as Protector of the kingdom did not end the bitter enmity between the Parliamentarians and Royalists. Even the Navy, small as it was, was divided in its loyalties, and during the Civil War almost half of the fleet decided in favour of King Charles by taking as its commander Prince Rupert, a nephew of the king. With the execution of King Charles, Prince Rupert and his fleet left the country and established a base at Kinsale, in southern Ireland, from where they carried out attacks on English merchant ships in the Channel. Cromwell, however was determined not to tolerate this defiance of his authority. He realised that if England were to regain her former glory as a sea power there must be a proper naval organisation and that, in the first place, Prince Rupert's fleet must be destroyed.

THE FIRST DUTCH WAR, 1652–54

Robert Blake

In 1649, by order of the Council of State which governed the kingdom, 'Generals-at-Sea' were appointed to take command of the Navy. The first to be appointed were Army officers – Colonels Popham, Blake and Deane. Robert Blake, especially, was a remarkable man, having already served with distinction as a soldier, represented his home town, Bridgwater, in Parliament, and in his earlier years looked after his father's shipping business with great skill. Blake set about to destroy the menace of Prince Rupert's fleet, and mounted a blockade outside the harbour at Kinsale. During bad weather Rupert managed to slip out, but Blake was quickly at his heels; and, after a long chase to Portugal and later right into the Mediterranean itself, the greater part of Rupert's fleet was driven on to the rocky coastline of southern Spain, near Cartagena. Cromwell had found in Robert Blake the resolute leader he needed. But this was only the beginning: Blake now set about the reorganisation of the Navy, before starting on his real problem – the defeat of the Dutch. The wages of seamen were raised, the quality of food was improved, prize money introduced – in fact, anything that could be done to attract British seamen back to British ships was given consideration. Very soon seamen joined the new Navy under their new leader, and although there were only a few ships, Blake's leadership was so inspiring that his seamen behaved as a team. With only thirteen ships Blake attacked a powerful Dutch fleet led by Admiral Tromp. The Dutch were escorting a convoy off the coast of Kent, when to their surprise they found themselves challenged by Blake. By superior gunnery and seamanship Blake outwitted the Dutch and scattered their fleet; and a few months later this success was carried further, when Blake defeated another Dutch admiral, De Witt, at the battle of the Kentish Knock, just off the Goodwin Sands. Many more battles were fought against the Dutch, and in all but one of them Blake was victorious. In the end the Dutch stranglehold of the English Channel was broken.

After the First Dutch War, Blake took a fleet to the Mediterranean, where he destroyed the ships of the Barbary pirates who had so often preyed upon the shipping of all nations. This action made the British Navy respected by all countries. Just before his death, when England intervened in a war between France and Spain, Blake destroyed a large Spanish fleet in the harbour of Santa Cruz, in the Canary Islands. After this victory he returned home, but died as his ship was entering Plymouth Sound.

Blake had restored the good reputation of the Navy. His genius for organisation, his methods of fighting, his leadership, all had proved successful. When the monarchy was restored in 1660 in the person of Charles II, the new king decided to model his navy on Blake's ideas. For the first time official recognition was given to a separate navy, a Royal Navy, although the control of it was entrusted to Parliament.

Samuel Pepys and his Naval Records

King Charles II gave the post of Lord High Admiral to his brother James, Duke of York. Among the latter's most valuable assistants in the Navy Office was Samuel Pepys, who held the post of Clerk of the Acts and was later appointed Secretary to the Admiralty. Pepys was the author of the celebrated diary, but equally important from the naval viewpoint are the thousands of official letters that he left behind. It is from these that we are able to picture the Royal Navy in the time of Charles II. Recruiting for the lower deck was on a voluntary basis, though when the need arose 'press gangs' were used to force men into service. Although impressment could be employed for either land or sea service, it came to be used almost entirely to secure recruits for the Navy. Seafaring men between 18 and 55 years of age were liable, with the exception of certain classes. Even sailors actually serving on board a merchantman could be seized, and thus vessels were sometimes left crewless. It was customary for the press gang to land from a warship, seize likely men, and convey them to the ship as prisoners. An ordinary seaman was paid 19 shillings per month – not much by today's standards, but reasonable pay for the time. Discipline was severe, but, judging by the crimes that were common, it had to be, for drunkenness, dishonesty, fraud and forgery were everyday offences among sailors.

Officers joined as midshipmen at about the age of 12 and could pass for lieutenant at the age of twenty, but if they failed their examinations they usually remained midshipmen for the rest of their lives. A lieutenant serving with distinction aboard a warship could be promoted to captain, as there was then no rank in between. There were, in addition, specialist officers, but these were not given much opportunity for promotion, and in seniority they ranked below the Lieutenant. Such officers included the Master, responsible for the ship's navigation; the Gunner, responsible for the ship's armament; the Purser,[1] who had control of the ship's provisions and pay tickets for the ship's company; the Surgeon, Chaplain and Schoolmaster, as well as the Boatswain and Carpenter.

Among the officers too, behaviour was at times very poor, for many instances are recorded in the writings of Pepys of drunkenness, forgery and falsification of accounts. Nevertheless, as with the lower deck, the punishment of those who were caught was very severe.

There were no regulations concerning uniform, though many sailors produced a rig of their own – a red cap, tarry jacket, baggy trousers, and buckled shoes. Officers wore the usual civilian dress of a 'gentleman' of the period. The only rules relating to uniform applied to the warship itself, describing the types of flags or pendants it should fly. Robert Blake, a soldier, had held the title of 'General-at-Sea', but this was changed during the reign of Charles II to 'Admiral' so as to distinguish the Navy from he Army. There were three kinds of admiral – Admiral of the Red, of the White and of the Blue, and each flew a red, white or blue flag accordingly. The Red squadron took its place in the centre, the most important position for the control of the whole fleet; the Admiral of the White, considered next in order of importance, led the fleet; while the Admiral of the Blue was in the rear. This seniority in admirals led to the introduction of the ranks Admiral, Vice-Admiral and Rear-Admiral, depending upon whether their squadrons were Red, White or Blue.

---

[1] See 'Pusser' pg 97

THE SECOND DUTCH WAR, 1665–67

Such was the Navy of the time of Charles II, when once again war broke out with the Dutch. Britain had been granted trading facilities in Bombay and this greatly annoyed Dutch traders, who already had trading interests in that area. To incense them further, an English fleet had taken New Amsterdam from the Dutch, renaming it New York. But in home waters the English had no leader of the calibre of Blake, while the Dutch on the other hand were well prepared for a sea campaign and had a powerful fleet. All the same, when the two forces met off Lowestoft the English gained the day.

But when the English sailors presented their pay tickets for conversion to cash at the Navy Pay Office in London, they found that there was no money forthcoming. Blake's reorganisation of the Navy and the First Dutch War had cost far more than was expected, and none was left for the payment of wages. As a result, disgruntled British seamen left their ships in the naval dockyards and once more offered their services to the Dutch. This was just what the famous Dutch Admiral De Ruyter had longed for, and he seized the opportunity. Under the guidance of English deserters he took his fleet up the Medway, captured three ships and destroyed three more by fire, the English flagship *Royal Charles* being taken to Holland – a grievous blow indeed to the Royal Navy.

THE THIRD DUTCH WAR, 1672–74

Although peace followed, it was not for long, for in 1672 war broke out with Holland for the third time. On this occasion we allied ourselves with France, who were already at war with the Dutch. It was a difficult time for Holland: on land she was faced with possible invasion by the powerful French armies, whilst at sea she faced the combined French and English fleets. The first problem the Dutch overcame by destroying their dykes and flooding their country. This forced the French army to retreat. At sea, in the two battles fought off Southwold, or Sole Bay, and the Texel against the Allied fleets, they ignored the French squadrons and concentrated their attacks on the British fleet. On both occasions, owing to the difficulties of language and signals, the French fleet took no part in the actions; and, having suffered heavy casualties, our own fleet was forced to withdraw. Peace was signed and the hand of friendship was offered to Holland, for it was becoming generally recognised in England that in the future the real danger would come not from Holland but from the growing power of France.

CHAPTER FOUR

The Century of Wars with France

The new enemy

In 1685 Charles II died and was succeeded on the throne by his brother James II. The new king, however, was a Roman Catholic, and as his reign threatened to produce a revival of religious conflict, Parliament invited the young Protestant prince William of Orange and his English wife Mary to jointly occupy the throne of England. The new king landed in England and James II fled to France. With a Dutch prince on the throne of England, friendship was cemented between the two countries after their three bitter wars. In any event the struggle against England had so weakened the Dutch that Holland had sunk to a second-class power and France took her place as the foremost land power in Europe.

There were three regions in which English and French interests conflicted – in North America, the West Indies and India; and two of the three were prominent in the events of each of the wars which followed in the period known as the 'Hundred years' struggle with France'. It must be remembered however, that in the intervals of peace between the wars – and even during the time of fighting – the progress of English colonisation was proceeding and the British Empire was growing and getting richer in every way. But that progress was so gradual that men did not notice it, and they only remembered the wars and battles.

THE WAR OF THE ENGLISH SUCCESSION, 1689–97

King Louis XIV of France gave every assistance to the exiled James II in the form of money and men in an effort to restore James to the throne of England, and the War of the English Succession[1] followed. An attempt to invade England from Ireland was defeated in 1690 by King William at the battle of Boyne; but the French had had a temporary success on the previous day, when they encountered an Anglo-Dutch fleet off Beachy Head, about eight of the Allied fleet being destroyed. Delighted with this success, the French monarch decided in 1692 on another attempt at an invasion of England – this time from Normandy. James II, with a French army, waited on the beaches while the French fleet

[1] Sometimes called the War of the League of Augsburg.

sought control of the Channel. Our own fleet was already at sea when the French fleet was sighted near Cape Barfleur, in the Cherbourg Peninsula. In the battle which followed the enemy squadrons separated and were pursued; and a few days later the fireships and boats of Vice-Admiral George Rooke's division destroyed twelve French ships at La Hougue, where they had run themselves into shallow water. Watching the spectacle from the shore was James II, and with this decisive English victory any hopes he had of returning as King of England faded with the dying flames from the burning French warships.

THE WAR OF THE SPANISH SUCCESSION, 1702–1713

In 1700 the King of Spain died. In his will he decreed that his throne should be occupied by the grandson of King Louis XIV of France; so by a stroke of the pen the whole of Spain and the Spanish Netherlands were to become French. Great Britain, seeing a serious menace in the growing power of France, joined in a league against her, and the War of the Spanish Succession broke out. John Churchill, Duke of Marlborough, led the allied English and Dutch armies with great success against the French in Europe, and victory followed victory. At sea, the Navy was charged with the duty of securing a new naval base on the Spanish coast, Cadiz having been selected as the most suitable. An English fleet and land force under Admiral Sir George Rooke made an unsuccessful attempt to take the port. Rooke then heard that fifty Spanish treasure ships had put into Vigo, a port on the north-west coast of Spain. This prize had greater appeal than a further risky attempt to take Cadiz, and so Rooke proceeded to Vigo. He was too ill to lead the attack in person and directed his second-in-command, Vice-Admiral Thomas Hopsonn, to break through the boom protecting the anchorage. Despite the strong defences, the Spaniards were quickly overcome and 20 million 'pieces of eight' were removed from the holds of the enemy ships.

It was indeed a wonderful prize, but Admiral Rooke had not solved the problem of a new English base. Rather than return home without accomplishing something in this direction, he decided to attack Gibraltar, a barren rock held by about 80 Spanish soldiers. The English and Dutch marines were landed near what is now the Neutral Ground. The Spanish batteries were attacked by seamen under Captains Hicks and Jumper, reinforced by others under Captain Whitaker. A fierce struggle for the Spanish gun positions followed, during the course of which the enemy sprang a mine, killing forty of our men. Relentlessly, however, the assailants pressed on, until the garrison was overwhelmed. The attacks made by our forces are described as having been brave beyond example; and the capture of Gibraltar was accomplished with the loss of only sixty lives. To this very day, the only battle honour retained by the Royal Marines is 'Gibraltar'.

Later, in 1708, Minorca, a small Spanish island off the east coast of Spain, was occupied as a second British naval base.

Admiral Benbow

While all these victories were taking place in Europe, smaller actions against the French were fought in the Caribbean area, in the West Indies, in one of the most memorable of which the celebrated Admiral Benbow figured. With seven ships, he was patrolling in West Indian waters when a French squadron of similar size was sighted. Benbow gave chase, but soon found himself alone, the rest of his squadron having been left behind. Despite this handicap, he continued to chase the enemy for two days, until owing to a change in the wind, he was able to get the French ships within range of his guns and bring them to action, Benbow actually boarding the leading enemy vessel. Although severely wounded in the face and arm, he still continued to fight; and later, when his right leg was shattered and he was carried below, he insisted upon being brought up again on deck so that he could direct the battle. Eventually the remainder of his ships arrived, but failed to carry out the order for a 'close action'. In such circumstances further fighting was impossible and the action was broken off by Benbow, who was furious at the conduct shown by some of his commanders. A few months after this battle the whole story was told at a court-martial back in England, when two of his commanders were found guilty of cowardice in action and were shot.

France was so exhausted by her defeats, both in the Netherlands and in Spain, that she signed a peace treaty with England, the terms of which allowed Britain to retain Minorca and Gibraltar, as well as the right to colonise Newfoundland and to carry on trading in the West Indies without French or Spanish interference.

THE WAR OF JENKINS'S EAR, 1739

After 26 years of peace a sea captain named Jenkins came to London to complain that while he was peacefully sailing about his business in the West Indies he was attacked by Spaniards, who boarded his ship and cut off one of his ears. Jenkins produced an ear in a bottle as he told the story before a packed House of Commons. This news created great public excitement in England and people everywhere clamoured for revenge against Spain. The opening of this 'War of Jenkins's Ear' marked the beginning of a period of warfare which continued with very short intervals for more than seventy years.

THE WAR OF THE AUSTRIAN SUCCESSION, 1740–1748

A few skirmishes between English and Spanish ships had already taken place in the West Indies when events in Europe forced England to declare war on France for the second time. The war broke out in 1744 over the question of the succession to the throne of Austria, and at once the frontier was in a blaze. England allied herself to Prussia, which country was already at war with France over the same question.

Admiral Vernon

In the preliminary phase of the war Admiral Edward Vernon was prominent. He was patrolling in the West Indies with six ships in an effort to bring enemy vessels to action. Just off Portobello, near Panama, he chased a few Spanish galleons into the harbour and then decided, despite his small force, to seize the port itself. Although the harbour was protected by a fortress, Vernon was certain that his own gunfire would prove more effective than that of the enemy. Under cover of a barrage, his seamen landed and stormed the fortress. His losses were very few – less than a dozen seamen. The news of this victory soon reached England, where Vernon was hailed as a national hero.

Admiral Lord Anson

Another British admiral, Lord Anson, won fame in a different way. When Anson was appointed to the *Centurion* he was a Captain (Commodore in command of six ships and two storeships). His orders were to proceed to the South Seas, and 500 land soldiers were to be embarked for possible shore operations. As fully-trained soldiers were not available, 500 Chelsea out-pensioners were drafted in lieu; but those that could (241 in number) managed to desert before sailing, and their places were filled by newly-recruited marines who were entirely untrained. Even though his crews were suffering from the dread disease scurvy, Anson managed to seize Spanish treasure to the value of £500 000 and, following the track of Sir Francis Drake, he took his own ship, the *Centurion*, on a voyage round the world which lasted four years.

At a later stage in the war, both Admiral Vernon and Admiral Anson saw service in home waters, where they commanded fleets which successfully stood in the way of a French invasion of England. In 1747 Anson defeated a French fleet escorting a convoy off Cape Finisterre and captured six enemy warships. Both France and England, however, found this war rather costly and, with nothing really settled, both countries agreed to a peace treaty.

THE SEVEN YEARS' WAR, 1756–63

England and France both knew that this period of peace was only a lull in the struggle and each began to get ready for the next round. In France great preparations went ahead for a full-scale invasion of England, while a strong French force assembled at Toulon, in the Mediterranean, for an attack on our new base at Minorca.

Admiral Byng and the Loss of Minorca

The opening years of the war were full of disaster for England. Admiral the Hon. John Byng was sent with a weak squadron to defend Minorca at all costs, but when he reached Gibraltar he learned that the island had already been occupied by the French and only a small British garrison at Port Mahon, the capital, was still holding out against the enemy. Byng immediately set sail to succour this garrison. As he approached the harbour of Port Mahon he saw a French fleet drawn up to oppose him. An engagement followed, but owing to some misunderstanding of signals, only half of Admiral Byng's fleet came into action. The French concentrated their fire on the masts and rigging of the British ships and then withdrew from the fight. Byng thus found himself in a difficult position, for in the disabled state of his ships he could not give chase to the enemy and in any case many of his casualties needed hospital treatment. In view of these circumstances Admiral Byng carried out temporary repairs and retired to Gibraltar, where both his ships and his wounded seamen received attention.

But Minorca was lost, and this news quickly reached England, where Byng was blamed for the loss of the base. He was relieved of his command and on his return was charged with 'neglect of duty in battle', tried, found guilty and condemned to death. Although the verdict included a strong recommendation to mercy, commercial interests in the City were against him; no excuses were taken into consideration and the king confirmed that the sentence must be carried out. And so one morning in March 1757 Admiral Byng knelt on the quarterdeck of a ship in Portsmouth Harbour to face a firing squad of Marines. His enemies were satisfied, the loss of Minorca had been avenged; but in reality the admiral had died a martyr, for it was known that he had been sacrificed to shield the inefficiency of the Government of the day. His death led, however, to drastic changes in the administration. William Pitt, who was to prove one of our greatest Prime Ministers, became head of the Government. He had the ability to concentrate on urgent matters and had a great enthusiasm for his task. Soon all members of the Government realised that they had a leader at last and they were all members of one team fighting for the defence of the British Empire.

In India, where French and British trading interests clashed, the British trading post at Calcutta had been taken by an Indian ruler. The English officials and their families were barbarously forced into a very small and unventilated prison, and by next morning most of them had perished from the heat and lack of air. This incident, known as the 'Black Hole of Calcutta', enraged public opinion at home. On the other side of the world, in Canada, French colonisation of the trading posts along the St. Lawrence river and elsewhere had prospered. Yet, in the face of all these setbacks, William Pitt set to work to revive the name of Britain.

1759 – THE YEAR OF VICTORIES

The tide of fortune did not turn at once, and Pitt had to work for nearly two years before he could bring about a victory. His plan was threefold – to frustrate a French invasion of England and to strike at the enemy in India and also in Canada.

Admiral Boscawen

To carry out his first objective Pitt decided that the best way was to prevent a link-up of the French Toulon fleet with their fleet based at Brest. Admiral Boscawen was given the duty of blockading the Toulon fleet, whilst Admiral Hawke carried out a watch on the enemy at Brest. Unfortunately, with the loss of Minorca Boscawen was obliged to base his fleet at Gibraltar; from where he kept a constant watch on shipping passing through the Strait. One afternoon the French Toulon fleet slipped through the Strait, but within a few hours Boscawen was at sea and by superb seamanship overtook the enemy and scattered their ships, capturing and destroying three.

Admiral Sir Edward Hawke at Quiberon Bay

Meanwhile Hawke, who had kept a watch during the summer months on the port of Brest in fair weather and foul, was forced to withdraw his squadron in the teeth of a gale. The enemy took advantage of the situation by coming out of the harbour, but even before the weather moderated Hawke gave chase. The French ships sought refuge in Quiberon Bay, on the coast of the Bay of Biscay. This is a particularly rocky coastline and requires very accurate navigation, and the French, with their local knowledge, knew the dangers well; but Hawke realised that his only chance of destroying the French fleet was to follow them into their refuge. Despite the fact that it was still blowing a whole gale, Hawke pursued the enemy into Quiberon Bay before nightfall, and by daylight next morning he had shattered the enemy ships with deadly gunfire. At very small cost to his own squadron – two ships were wrecked – Hawke thus gave the final blow to French hopes of invasion.

The Capture of Quebec

To fulfil part of his second plan, to attack the enemy abroad, Pitt chose a young British commander, General James Wolfe, and gave him a well-equipped force to strike at the important French capital of Canada – Quebec. Admiral Charles Saunders was charged with the transport of Wolfe's army, and by September 1759 the English ships had sailed up the St. Lawrence and were all under the walls of the great fortress of Quebec, which looked down upon them from lofty cliffs. The ships' guns could do little harm by firing at the walls so high above them, and Wolfe realised that to capture the city he would have to get at his enemy by land, and that to do this he must effect a landing upstream from the city. Complete surprise was essential, and in order to deceive the enemy regarding his intentions, Wolfe got Admiral Saunders to take his fleet in daylight beyond Quebec, which made the French believe that the English fleet had decided to attack one of their smaller settlements farther upstream. But as night fell Admiral Saunders anchored his ships, and silently, Wolfe's army was rowed ashore to the foot of the cliffs. Once ashore, a path up the cliffside was discovered, and up this path, with all their equipment, the soldiers scrambled. The next morning, the astonished French army found themselves forced to a battle. A bayonet charge drove the French soldiers in headlong flight over the Plains of Abraham into Quebec itself, and although General Wolfe was slain in the action, our soldiers were victorious and Quebec – the gateway to Canada – was ours. England rejoiced at the great victories of Hawke at Quiberon Bay and Wolfe in Canada, and the toast of London was 'May all our commanders have the eye of a Hawke and the heart of a Wolfe!' Many songs were composed in honour of the great victories; but one in particular, 'Heart of Oak', was destined to become one of the most popular in the fleet.

Even before these glorious victories the new Prime Minister had taken steps to avenge the 'Black Hole of Calcutta': in 1757 Robert Clive won the great battle of Plassey, and Bengal became a part of the British Empire. And in the years that followed the 'Year of Victories' many more French and Spanish islands in the West Indies were captured.

Pitt had proved himself an inspiring leader, with a rare ability for selecting the right men for the job. While his enemies were fully occupied by land wars in Europe, he had sent brilliant young leaders abroad to strike at the enemy in their far-distant possessions. It was really a triumph of good administration and well-directed bravery that marked the expansion of the British Empire during the time of William Pitt.

But in 1760 a new king, George III, came to the throne, and when fresh dangers arose and Britain's successes seemed likely to make other nations turn against her, the king felt that Pitt was going too far and that we ought to make peace. So Pitt was dismissed and a peace treaty was signed with France. It provided that English colonisation of Canada and America should continue without interference from either France or Spain, and at the same time decreed many of the islands in the Spanish West Indies should become British. Both Spain and France regarded the peace treaty as a disgrace and were determined to have their revenge as soon as they could.

THE QUARREL WITH THE AMERICAN COLONISTS

To protect our colonies in America, British regiments were kept there; for this, of course, money had to be provided. At home, however, the king's new ministers were very much troubled by the large debts which had accumulated as a result of the Seven Years' War. Parliament decided, therefore, that the colonists themselves should pay something towards the expenses of British protection. A small tax was imposed on them in the way of stamps used on official documents. But the Government was very unwise in deciding to do this without getting the colonists to agree beforehand, for the colonists had always declared that they could only be taxed with their own consent.

There was trouble, also, over the question of trade. By the Navigation Laws our American colonists were not allowed to trade directly with foreign countries – all their exports had first to pass through British ports. The Government now proposed to levy a duty on rum and molasses imported into New England from the Spanish West Indies and from which the colonists manufactured rum for export. As with the stamp duty, the colonists resented this trade imposition and went in for smuggling on a large scale. The cost of providing Customs officers to stamp out smuggling kept growing, and only added to the burden of providing yet more money for the maintenance of law and order. The British Government therefore decided that a firm hand must be taken, that full duties on molasses should be collected and that, once and for all, smuggling must be stopped. This led to serious trouble, especially in Boston, where many colonists made their living by smuggling. Here the colonists rioted and threw into Boston harbour hundreds of chests of tea destined for the colony.

The colonists withstood all British demands, and in 1775 war began in earnest. This presented Britain with the problem of reinforcing and supplying her armies across so many thousands of miles of ocean. The colonists found a great leader in George Washington, and very quickly became a well-organised force. Meanwhile Spain and France, delighted to see England in trouble, joined in the war on the side of the American colonists. So we were faced with the problems of a land war in America and a war at sea against both France and Spain.

Admiral Viscount Keppel

A small English fleet was kept in American waters, whilst at home 55 men-of-war were put under the command of Admiral Keppel to protect our shores. In July 1778 Keppel met a French fleet off Ushant and, like Admiral Byng of earlier days, found that the French concentrated their broadsides on the masts and rigging of his ships. Once these were destroyed, the French withdrew out of range and Admiral Keppel found himself in the unhappy position of being unable to give chase to the enemy. On his return Keppel was charged with 'breaking off the action', a report which was quite false. He was tried by court-martial, but acquitted amid the jubilation of his friends, who chaired him through the streets of Portsmouth. To this day his name is commemorated by a hotel on the Hard at Portsmouth called 'Keppel's Head'.

It was on the mainland of America, however, that the outcome of the war was really decided. The French sent troops to assist the colonists in their struggle, while since the Seven Years' War our own navy had been so sadly neglected that we had insufficient ships in commission to blockade the French ports. Besides this, there were too few fast sailing ships and frigates to protect our merchant ships against the French fleet which was operating off the American coast.

Lord Cornwallis, the British army commander, found the colonists' forces too strong for him and he was forced to retreat to the seaport base of Yorktown, where he hoped to find reinforcements and supplies from the British fleet. But there was no British fleet to welcome him, for our own naval commander, Admiral Graves, had been intercepted by a French fleet under De Grasse. Once again the French employed their peculiar method of fighting, and the British fleet was left crippled aloft. With no hope of escape or relief, our armies in America were forced to capitulate.

The Battle of the Saints

Admiral Sir George Rodney, who was commanding a British fleet in the West Indies at this period, did manage to bring de Grasse to action, however, and thus avenged the defeat of Admiral Graves. Early in 1782 Rodney encountered the French fleet just off the group of islands in the West Indies known as the Saints. The French did not want to fight, as they were on their way to invade Jamaica, but Rodney overtook the enemy and prepared for battle. For a while both fleets deployed on opposite tacks in readiness, when quite suddenly Rodney noticed a slight change in the direction of the wind. He immediately altered course and cut through the enemy line. This sudden and unexpected move demoralised the French and five of their ships were taken before they could escape.

Rodney did much to restore our naval strength and prestige, but the surrender of our army at Yorktown had already given the colonists victory, and in the peace treaty which followed, in 1783, we agreed to recognise their independence and were obliged to give up some of our possessions in the West Indies.

Captain Cook's Voyages

Although the victory of the colonists meant the loss of America, events were going on elsewhere which showed that Britain was still a force to be reckoned with, particularly at sea. While the war with the colonists was still in progress, Lieutenant James Cook, a farmer's son, was exploring the new lands of Australia and New Zealand on behalf of England. He had already shown his capabilities as a navigator by assisting to chart the St. Lawrence River before General Wolfe's attack on Quebec. In his new venture his ship, the *Endeavour*, rounded Cape Horn and then sailed across the Pacific to New Zealand, which had already been discovered by a Dutch explorer named Tasman. Cook, however, spent six months charting the islands and discovered far more about them than Tasman had done. He also explored much of the coastline of Australia, and wherever he landed he planted the British flag and claimed the land in the name of the king. For these achievements he was promoted Commander and later Captain. Afterwards he made two more voyages of exploration, only to lose his life in a fight with natives in Hawaii. His writings and charts remain as a fascinating record of his work. In addition to his navigational skill, he was a man of advanced ideas and found that the sailor's disease, 'scurvy', could be overcome by a diet of vegetables, either pickled or in the form of soup.

So, although we had lost America, both Rodney and Cook showed the world that the skill of British seamanship was still alive – and, at the same time, that Britain could build up an Empire in new countries.

CHANGES IN THE GEORGIAN NAVY

During the reigns of the Georges many changes took place in the Royal Navy. In 1748 a uniform was introduced for officers. At first rank was shown by buttons, but later gold lace was introduced – three rows denoting a full admiral. Seamen were permitted to purchase clothing from the 'pusser', although no definite uniform regulations were enforced. Nevertheless the lower deck conformed to their own type of uniform, a round blue jacket, white trousers, spotted shirt and buckled shoes, while on their heads they often sported a tarred hat upon which the name of their ship was displayed.

The food on board was still of poor quality; pork, beef, cheese, ship's biscuits – all appeared on the ration scale, but more often than not the meat was bad and the biscuit was alive with maggots. These maggots hatched out into insects called weevils and there is evidence that even weevil-infected biscuits were eaten by our seamen, for it is recorded that they had a bitter taste. To stomach such food needed quite a lot of courage! The daily rum ration was half a pint. Naturally, with such a liberal issue there was much drunkenness, so much so that Admiral Vernon ordered the rum should be issued diluted with water. From that day rum mixed with water was known as 'grog', after the nickname of Admiral Vernon – 'Old Grogram' – who was so called because he often wore a waterproof cloak made of grogram. Until the rum issue was abolished a sailor who drew his rum ration was referred to in the ledger as 'G' or 'Grog'.

Only about one-quarter of the seamen were volunteers, the remainder being made up of 'pressed men' and the unwanted from prisons. Most ships' companies were, in consequence, a very mixed bunch; rogues, thieves, vagabonds, smugglers, embezzlers – all were numbered among the crews of HM Fleet. It is therefore not surprising that in order to achieve some measure of discipline among such a variety, punishments, even for minor offences, were still severe. Up to six dozen lashes with a cat-o'-nine-tails were sometimes awarded for drunkenness.

Ships, too, had changed. Ships of the line were known as 1st, 2nd or 3rd rates, depending upon the number of guns (100–64) carried; they had three or two gun decks. Frigates (the 'eyes of the fleet') were rated as 5th and 6th rates, and had only one gun deck. A 4th rate (two-deck) came between these two main classes. All were commanded by post captains. In 1782, a ship called the *Royal George* was tragically lost at Spithead. As a result of the inquiry which followed the disaster, it was discovered that the timbers in her bottom were very much decayed, but the necessary repairs had been postponed owing to dockyard economy. The evil effects of the teredo worm on ships' bottoms had always been a serious menace and various forms of sheathing had been tried in the past to cure their ravages but it was not until about 1750, that the trouble was overcome by the introduction of copper sheathing. Besides resisting the teredo worm, this had the effect of reducing the accumulation of weed on a ship's bottom and of improving her sailing qualities.

A new type of gun known as a 'carronade' was carried in Georgian ships. This gun took its name from the Carron Works near Glasgow, where it was first produced. It was a short weapon which fired both solid shot and grapeshot, and it proved very deadly in close-range fighting.

Signalling, too, had not been neglected. It had been painfully obvious in many actions that defeat might have been turned into victory had the admiral in command known exactly what was going on in every ship in his fleet. Admiral Kempenfelt devised a system of signalling by using nine flags which enabled ships three or four miles apart to 'talk' to each other.

The health of sailors also showed a great improvement, largely because of the efforts of Captain Cook, who had been so successful in overcoming scurvy. Dr. Lind, who was in charge of the new Naval Hospital at Haslar near Gosport took up this study and eventually found that the issue of lemon juice to sailors prevented the disease.

In the realm of navigation, too, great strides had been made. Even in the time of Columbus latitude could be fixed fairly accurately, but no accurate method of determining longitude had been discovered until the time of Captain Cook, who took several watches with him on his voyages in order to find a reliable timekeeper, which is a necessity if longitude is to be fixed with accuracy. One such timepiece, made by John Harrison, lost only seven minutes in a voyage of three years, and this instrument – the first marine chronometer – still ticks away gayly in the National Maritime Museum at Greenwich.

Another important change took place in the Navy in Georgian days. For many years the guns of warships had been cast by smelting iron with charcoal. But the continual use of charcoal in such very large quantities led in time to the wholesale destruction of our forests, and a new method had to be found. This was discovered in the use of coal, and Northern England, where both coal and iron were found side by side, soon became a thickly-populated manufacturing area. Newly-invented machinery enabled goods to be produced more quickly and in greater quantities, and with the invention of the steam engine a new industrial age opened, known as the Industrial Revolution. Years later this was to affect the sailing ship very profoundly.

CHAPTER FIVE

The Struggle against Revolutionary France

In 1789 the eyes of the world were turned towards France, where a violent social upheaval was beginning. The people of that country had been heavily taxed and oppressed for many years by the nobility, till at last, unable to stand any more of this treatment, they rose against their masters. Very quickly they got the upper hand, and in 1793 the king and queen of France, as supreme representatives of the nobility, were seized by the mob and executed. Thirsty for more blood, the revolutionists erected guillotines throughout France and thousands of the French aristocracy met the same fate as their king and queen.

At first people in England were inclined to sympathise with the revolutionists, but when the new French Republican armies overran Belgium and Holland and threatened to send 50 000 revolutionaries to rid England of her monarchy, ideas in England quickly changed. Both Austria and Prussia, alarmed by the strength and success of the Republican armies under their newly-found and brilliant leader Napoleon Bonaparte, declared war against revolutionary France; England also, horrified at the murder of the French monarch and the possibility of a French invasion, joined them.

Lord Howe and 'the Glorious First of June'

England could not hope to do much with her small army – after all, the population of this land was then only nine million compared with the 25 million people in France. And so, very wisely, England decided to put her faith in her navy and use this as her contribution to the war. Admiral Howe, who had already served with distinction in Hawke's action at Quiberon Bay, was given the duty of blockading the French fleet at Brest. He found this harbour empty of shipping and immediately began a search for the enemy, who, having sailed to escort in a large grain convoy from America, was discovered some 400 miles west of Brest.

After two partial engagements on 28th and 29th May, followed by two days of fog, Howe was able on 1st June 1794 to bring the French fleet to close action, the enemy being to leeward. His intention was for all ships to pass through the enemy's line and to engage them from leeward, but this was not done in all cases and the fighting was on both sides. The result was the complete disorganisation of the enemy, in which six of the French ships were captured and one was sunk. It was a signal triumph for England – and for Lord Howe in particular, who was 69 years of age at the time.

The Battle of Cape St. Vincent, 1797

Meanwhile in the Mediterranean a watch was kept on the French fleet based at Toulon. Admiral Lord Hood, who was charged with this task, found it a difficult one, since his nearest base was at Gibraltar, hundreds of miles away. A nearer base had to be found, and it was decided to occupy Corsica, the nearest island to France. In these operations he was assisted by Captain Horatio Nelson in the *Agamemnon*, who damaged the sight of his right eye at the siege of Calvi.

The new base was not held for long, however, for events in Europe greatly changed the whole situation. Napoleon Bonaparte, France's 'petit caporal', taught his armies to strike swiftly and to live off the spoils of the conquered lands. In a very short period his armies, in lightning marches and attacks, defeated Austria. Spain, with her large fleet, decided to ally herself with France. As this meant a watch on Spanish ports, orders were given to Admiral Sir John Jervis, who in 1796 was commander-in-chief in the Mediterranean, to move his fleet to Lisbon, in Portugal, since that country remained friendly to the British cause. From this base Admiral Jervis blockaded the Spanish fleet in their harbour at Cadiz in order to prevent a link-up of the French Mediterranean and Spanish fleets, which, it was suspected, were to be used for the invasion of England. For two years the blockade of Cadiz was enforced, until in February 1797 Admiral Jervis, with fifteen ships, sighted just off Cape St. Vincent a Spanish fleet of twenty-five vessels making for Cadiz. The two divisions of the enemy were some distance apart, and Jervis steered in a single line between them. At one period it appeared that the Spaniards might escape, until Nelson, against orders, swung out of line and put his ship in the path of the enemy. Although he had but 74 guns, he did not hesitate to attack the biggest Spanish warship of 130 guns. Nelson himself boarded two enemy warships and took part in very close fighting. The battle resulted in a great victory for England and one that was needed. Sir John Jervis was created Earl of St. Vincent and Nelson was made a Knight of the Bath, and not long afterwards he was promoted to flag rank, in recognition of the victory.

The Naval Mutinies

Within a few months of this battle, however, two separate mutinies occurred at home. The first broke out at Portsmouth, where the sailors refused to go to sea. They were dissatisfied with their pay, which had not been increased for many years, with their food, and with their long periods on board without leave. Admiral Howe, the respected victor of the Glorious First of June, was sent down from London to Portsmouth to talk to the seamen. He understood their complaints and grievances and knew the truth behind them, and on his authorisation the Government promised to meet the sailors' demands. Yet within a month or so another mutiny occurred, this time at The Nore. The causes of this second mutiny were mainly political, for most of the sailors' grievances had already been remedied as a result of the Portsmouth mutiny. The leader of The Nore revolt was an ex-midshipman named Richard Parker, who felt he had a grievance against his former service. He was a good speaker and was quick to round up as his supporters many disgruntled sailors.

Admiral Duncan and the Battle of Camperdown, 1797

Unhappily for England the Nore mutiny took place at an awkward time. At the island of Texel, on Holland's doorstep, the Scottish Admiral Duncan was blockading the French-controlled Dutch fleet, which was also intended for the invasion of England. When the news of the Nore mutiny reached Duncan's fleet, many of his sailors decided to join forces with the Nore mutineers and Duncan soon found himself with but two ships. In spite of this unexpected handicap, he used these vessels to advantage. Maintaining his position close off Texel, Duncan stationed his one remaining consort at horizon distance, where she made fictitious flag signals. This gave the enemy the impression that other British ships were stationed just below the horizon. By the time the Dutch fleet came out the Nore mutiny was over, the ringleaders had been hanged, and Duncan's disaffected ships had rejoined him. Just off the small Dutch coastal village of Camperdown a battle lasting some five hours was fought, until the Dutch admiral hauled down his flag in surrender. The victories of Cape St. Vincent and Camperdown were the salvation of England, for they prevented the union of the enemy fleets; but it might well have been a different story if Duncan's tremendous bluff had not been so successful.

THE FIGHT AGAINST NAPOLEON

Nelson and the Battle of the Nile, 1798

Having failed to win command of the seas, the French devised another scheme to injure Britain, this time by striking a blow at the British possessions in India. Bonaparte with his armies had proved himself almost the master of Europe, but he found the British navy a formidable obstacle; in fact, the war with France has often been called 'the struggle between the elephant and the whale'. As the invasion of England had been stopped by the Royal Navy, he decided to strike at our possessions in India. He therefore planned to invade Egypt and then use that country as his base for the attack on India. The Government was unaware of this new French project, although the Admiralty was a little suspicious of what might be going on in the Mediterranean. Nelson, who had been taking part in the continued blockade of Spanish ports and islands, was ordered by St. Vincent to investigate Santa Cruz where a treasure ship was thought to be lying. In a night attack on Teneriffe, the largest of the Spanish-held Canary Islands, Nelson had lost his right arm; he had already damaged his right eye, and so he was a figure to be remembered. He was of only frail physique and quite frequently he was seasick, yet despite all his physical handicaps, his leadership, his devotion to his men and above all his great sense of duty, all proved an inspiration to his seamen. His own ship's company thought the world of him, and history records that during the naval mutinies not one man under his command took part in them.

In the following year, 1798, St. Vincent learnt that a fleet was being prepared by the enemy at Toulon, and he selected Nelson to go in quest of it. Nelson took his squadron into the Mediterranean, where he found the harbour of Toulon empty. He sensed that the French had sailed eastwards, so, with every sail hoisted, Nelson followed. Whilst off the Italian coast he pieced together bits of information given him by fishermen, and correctly deduced that the French fleet was making for Alexandria. He made good progress, and actually passed within 60 miles of the French invasion fleet without realising that he was so near. Having got ahead of the French, he found Alexandria empty and so continued his search, but wherever he went he drew a blank. He then retraced his track past the island of Crete and sailed back towards Sicily, where he revictualled.

By this time Bonaparte had landed in Egypt, having taken the island of Malta en route, from the Knights of St. John. Within a few weeks Bonaparte had taken Cairo and subdued Egypt. As soon as Nelson heard this news he again shaped course for Alexandria, and on the 1st August 1798 he received a signal from his leading vessel that there were thirteen French men-of-war in Aboukir Bay, a few miles east of Alexandria. This bay, at the mouth of the Nile, is made dangerous by invisible shoals. The French, under the command of Admiral Brueys, had anchored their ships in a curved formation. Nelson divided his own fleet so that one section under Captain Foley, in the *Goliath*, could get on the shore side of the enemy, whilst he in his flagship, the *Vanguard*, could attack from seaward. A gap was noticed between a buoy marking the verge of a shoal and the stern of the first French ship. Through this small gap Captain Foley daringly led his ships, and just before darkness the signal was given to open fire. Although Nelson's fleet was the same size as the French, so effective was the attack from two sides at once that only two of the French ships of the line and two frigates escaped destruction. This brilliant victory isolated Bonaparte and his armies in Egypt without any means of escape – nor could reinforcements be sent from France, for the battle of the Nile gave Nelson complete control of the Mediterranean. To add to his battle scars Nelson received a wound in the forehead during the action. A splinter of iron struck him above his damaged eye, causing the flesh to hang over the lid. The splinter was removed and the wound stitched. Although it healed, a nasty scar was left and, typical of Nelson, he trained a lock of hair to cover the scar so that it might not attract too much attention.

There was great rejoicing in England at this signal victory over the French, but it was not until 1800 that the small French garrison in Malta capitulated. With the absence of Bonaparte in Egypt events in Europe went against France and her soldiers were gradually expelled from Italy and Germany. When this news reached Bonaparte he realised that only his presence in France could save his country. He managed to elude the British blockade in Egypt and, leaving his armies behind him, escaped back to France in a frigate. By June 1800 – so great was his genius as a soldier – he had raised new armies, reconquered Italy by marching his men over the Alps via the St. Bernard Pass, defeated the Austrians and forced the Russians to withdraw from the war against him. Once again his menace overshadowed Europe. He forced Russia, Denmark and Sweden to join in what was called the 'Armed Neutrality of the Northern Powers' – which meant that the countries concerned were forbidden to trade with Great Britain.

The Battle of Copenhagen, 1801

Britain had traded with the Baltic countries for centuries and she did not intend that this trade should cease on Bonaparte's orders. A fleet was at once assembled under Admiral Sir Hyde Parker, with Nelson, a much junior admiral, as second-in-command. In March 1801 the fleet sailed for Copenhagen as an effective force to make the Danes continue their trade with England. Strong forts protected the harbour entrance and uncharted shoals made the passage of the channel a tricky feat of navigation. Nelson took some shallow-draught ships through the narrow channel during darkness. He positioned his squadron so well that the Danish fleet was between it and the enemy's shore batteries. The action, however, went on for a long time and Admiral Parker, sensing that something was wrong, hoisted a signal for the recall of Nelson. When this was received aboard the *Elephant*, Nelson's ship, he moved the stump of his right arm in a manner which always denoted great emotion and, putting the telescope to his blind eye, remarked, 'I really do see the signal' – and so the action continued. In trying to reinforce their ships by ferrying more men from the shore the Danes suffered great slaughter, so much so that Nelson sent a message on shore stating that he did not wish to destroy more Danish lives, but if they persisted in fighting he would bombard Copenhagen itself. So peace terms were agreed, and Nelson had one more victory to his credit.

A change of Prime Minister at home brought a temporary peace between England and France, but it was obvious that Bonaparte had set his heart on the invasion of England and was using the breathing space to mass his armies round Dunkirk and Boulogne, ready for the invasion. 'The Channel is but a ditch', he remarked, 'and anyone can cross it who has but the courage to try'. Faced with the threat of an invasion by 150 000 French soldiers, Britain declared war on France after only thirteen months of peace.

In 1804 Bonaparte was proclaimed Emperor, and thenceforth he is usually referred to by his Christian name.

Nelson and Collingwood – Trafalgar, 1805

Napoleon had set his mind on a quick and easy victory over Great Britain, and from his headquarters at Boulogne he gathered thousands of flat-bottomed boats to transport his vast army across the Channel. To do this he needed control of the Channel for 24 hours, in which time he believed his armies could cross. He intended that his Mediterranean fleet should join up with the Spanish fleet at Cadiz and that this strong combination would then make for the West Indies, as if to attack our colonies there. But the real object of this demonstration was to entice Nelson, who was certain to give chase when he found their route led away from Europe and the English Channel. Napoleon's intention was that his huge fleet, on reaching the West Indies, should turn sharply on its tracks and steer for Brest, where they would overcome the British blockade of the port and thus free another large French fleet. Then this huge armada was to sail up the Channel, crush any British resistance and so safeguard the crossing of the French invasion armies. Blockading the port of Brest were Admiral Cornwallis and Admiral Collingwood, while in the Mediterranean Nelson kept watch on Toulon.

The Great Chase

The first part of Napoleon's elaborate plan worked well, for the French fleet under Admiral Villeneuve escaped from Toulon in rough weather when Nelson's fleet was blown away from its normal blockading area. Villeneuve reached Cadiz and with the Franco-Spanish fleet made for the West Indies. As soon as Nelson discovered this escape he gave chase, although the enemy had such a start that there was no hope of overtaking them; at the same time he despatched a fast sloop to England to warn the Admiralty of the danger. On receipt of this news, part of the fleet blockading Brest was put under the command of Admiral Calder and detached to intercept the enemy. In point of fact, Villeneuve, having lured Nelson away from the Mediterranean, returned with his fleet to Europe, only to find his way barred by Admiral Calder. After an indecisive action in a mist, Villeneuve put into Vigo, a port in north-west Spain. So Napoleon heard to his disgust and rage that the fleet which was to enable him to cross the Channel had failed to appear. Moreover, when it came out of Vigo it headed, not northwards to the Channel, but southwards to Cadiz to get more supplies and reinforcements. Napoleon despatched a letter accusing Villeneuve of lack of courage and blaming him for the failure of the invasion. Nelson meanwhile, having failed to contact the enemy, returned home to seek orders to destroy the enemy fleet once and for all; and, having received the required instructions, and with Collingwood as second in command, he undertook the blockade of Cadiz.

Villeneuve, who had been stung to the quick by the letter from Napoleon, plucked up courage and decided to come out of the harbour and make a fight of it. He knew Nelson well, for he was one of the few survivors of the Battle of the Nile. On 19th October 1805 the 33 ships of Villeneuve's squadron came out of Cadiz and set a southerly course. Nelson, whose plans were already made, had 27 ships; these he kept over the horizon, and not until dawn on the 21st October did he show his fleet to the enemy, just off Cape Trafalgar. Nelson's plan was that his fleet should be divided into two independent commands, one under Collingwood, who was to attack the rear of the long-drawn-out enemy line, while Nelson would concentrate on the centre and the van. Collingwood was in action first, followed a mile away by Nelson in his flagship the *Victory*. By all the principles of gunnery the *Victory* should not have reached the enemy line, for whilst approaching she was fully exposed to the broadsides of Villeneuve's fleet. But even though the mizzen mast and the wheel of the *Victory* were shot away, Nelson continued his dangerous course towards the enemy. On the approach of the *Victory* the enemy closed up the line, so that the bows of each ship were almost touching the stern of the ship ahead. Nelson, in full dress uniform, gave orders to open fire just as the *Victory* crashed its way between two French vessels, the *Bucentaure* and the *Redoutable*. With a terrific onslaught, the hundred guns of the *Victory* raked the decks of the two Frenchmen as she smashed through the gap, but in this moment of triumph Nelson himself received a mortal would from a French sniper in the mizzen top of the *Redoutable*. With his face covered so that his men might not recognise him, he was carried below, where for four hours, though in great pain, he made constant enquiries about the action. His last signal, which remained flying throughout, was 'Engage the enemy more closely'. With twenty ships destroyed and 2800 of the enemy killed, compared with our loss of 429, the wisdom of his signal was beyond doubt, but the nation mourned the death of a man whose name was a household word. His body was brought home to England, and in January of the following year it was laid to rest in St. Paul's Cathedral. Thirty-one admirals and 100 captains, together with the crew of the *Victory*, followed the body of their dead hero to its final resting-place.

The war against France lasted another ten years, but it was chiefly a land war, for everywhere at sea the British Navy was supreme. Napoleon was forced to abdicate in 1814 and was exiled to the island of Elba, in the Mediterranean. In 1815, however, he escaped and returned to France, where, once again on the throne and master of an army, he made preparations for the decisive campaign which should settle the fate of Europe. Great Britain and her allies had also a powerful army on the Continent, under the supreme command of the great Duke of Wellington; and on 18th June the opposing forces met at Waterloo, a village not far from Brussels, where, after a battle that lasted most of the day, the French were put to flight and Napoleon's ambitious designs came to an end. He was once more sent into exile, this time to the remote island of St. Helena, in the South Atlantic, and there he died in 1821. There is no doubt that the genius of Nelson and British sea-power were among the main causes of his defeat.

After Trafalgar the British Navy remained supreme for over 100 years – Britain was truly 'Mistress of the Seas'. In 1816 British naval prestige was raised even higher when Viscount Exmouth dealt a final blow to the many pirates that operated from the north African coastline. Their base at Algiers was bombarded from the sea for five hours until the ruler of the city agreed to our terms. Over 3000 slaves were liberated as a result of Lord Exmouth's action and ships of all nations could proceed on their lawful trading without the constant threat of piratical attacks.

CHAPTER SIX

From Sail to Steam, from Wood to Iron

The Screw Propeller

Queen Victoria came to the throne in 1837 and reigned for sixty-three years. Her reign was marked by an enormous expansion of our export trade, the coming of railways, the invention of the telegraph and telephone, and the growth of the British Empire. Her reign saw many changes in the navy, too. The most important of these was the change from sail to steam, which proved to be a very gradual process. Early steam ships were propelled by paddles, and their use as warships would have meant a reduction in the number of guns carried on the broadside, since the paddles took up a lot of space. At first the Admiralty experimented with a paddle-driven tug called the *Alecto*, but when a screw-driven vessel was produced, a tug of war between the *Alecto* and a new screw-driven tug, the *Rattler*, proved the screw-driven vessel the stronger of the two. With such a vessel, it was agreed, there would be no interference with the positioning of the broadside guns; but admirals of the old school maintained that such a ship, using dirty coal as fuel, would never be clean. All these excuses only delayed the change-over, although a combination of sail and steam was tried. This type of vessel was fitted with a retractable or lifting screw as well as being fully rigged for sailing. The screw was used to get the ship in and out of harbour, but once at sea the order 'Down funnel and up screw' was given, when the vessel became a true sailing ship.

The Ironclad

It was not until 1854, during the Crimean War, that the real value of the steam-driven vessel was fully appreciated. This war was fought against Russia, and this time we had France as our ally. In an attack against the Russian fortress of Sebastopol a new projectile, the shell, was used by the Russians and showed that wooden ships offered no protection against the heavier weight of explosive which the shells carried. Some new and stronger protection was needed for a battleship, and so the iron ship, or 'ironclad', soon replaced the 'wooden walls of England'. The first all-metal battleship, with a hull thick enough to withstand the new type of projectile, was the *Warrior*, which made her appearance in 1860. Her main armament was changed from time to time, but in 1861 it comprised twenty-six 68-pounder muzzle-loading and ten 110-pounder breech-loading guns.

The Turret

Further experiment led to the rifling of the barrel; this permitted a heavier gun, breech-loading but firing with greater accuracy and range than any known before. At the time of Trafalgar the *Victory* could fire a 32-lb shot a distance of 1½ miles, but the new breech-loading gun, only eighty years later, could fire a shell of about eight hundredweight a distance of nearly five miles! With such a heavy weight of shell there was no need for a warship to carry so many small guns, and as the new vessels built of iron could stand heavier weights, the new guns were mounted in turrets which could be revolved to train on any angle. Slowly the change took place from sail to steam, from wooden to iron ships, from small muzzle-loaders to powerful breech-loading, shell-firing guns. The first ship to deserve the name of a modern battleship was the *Devastation*, built in 1873, for she had all the new developments – an iron hull, screw propulsion and 25-ton guns in turrets. She had no sails, but carried two sets of steam propelling machinery. Her displacement was 9300 tons and she had a speed of 14 knots.

New Naval Ranks

These changes brought with them many other innovations. The most interesting newcomer was the Engineer, who was required to look after the 'steam boilers'. When the importance of this new branch was fully appreciated an Engineering College was opened at Keyham in 1880. In 1869 the former Master of a ship was given a commission as a Navigating Lieutenant, and the rank of Sub-Lieutenant was again substituted for that of Mate. He wore one gold stripe and all other stripes had to be adjusted, and so the modern system of officers' ranks came into being. The Purser became the Paymaster in 1844, and, with the greater importance given to religion, Chaplains of all denominations were permitted to hold commissions in the fleet. In 1853 a Continuous Service Scheme was introduced to make service in the navy an attractive proposition: and, with greater religious influence and a better type of recruit, drunkenness and other petty crimes diminished. In consequence, the scale of punishment was greatly reduced, and in 1866 it was embodied in the Naval Discipline Act.

Naval Uniform

In 1857 new recruits were given a uniform which earned them the name of 'bluejackets'. This uniform was a double-breasted monkey jacket of blue serge, bell-bottomed trousers of the same material and a wide straw hat with a ribbon round it displaying the name of their ship. In 1869, at the express wish of Queen Victoria, beards were worn (but not moustaches). Her idea was that officers and men of the navy should be distinguished from those of the army, many of whom wore moustaches. Henceforth all naval officers and men were to be either clean-shaven or bearded. Despite the attractions offered by the Continuous Service Scheme – a ten-year contract with better pay, opportunities of promotion to Petty Officer and Warrant Officer and good gratuities – it took time before a sufficient number of volunteers came forward. Within a few years, however, naval service proved so popular that the navy has never since lacked recruits.

The Torpedo and the Submarine

The first weapons known as 'torpedoes' were underwater explosive charges without any independent means of locomotion and were, in fact, simply buoyant mines. But with the invention of the compressed air engine it became possible to devise a weapon that could travel independently under the water and convey an explosive charge to a selected target. The first true locomotive torpedo was invented by Robert Whitehead in 1866 and was a novel and formidable weapon. It could be fired from a small, fast 'torpedo-boat' to strike a battleship at its weakest part – the thin plating of the hull below the armour-plated belt. The attempt to counter this new weapon led to the development of the 'torpedo-boat destroyer', the forerunner of the modern destroyer and frigate, which was a very vast vessel armed with quick-firing guns and torpedoes and designed to cripple a torpedo-boat before the latter could fire its torpedoes at a battleship. As long as a battleship was protected or screened by destroyers there was little chance of its being struck by a torpedo – or so it appeared until the introduction of the submarine. This new craft could fire torpedoes while submerged, both by day and night. However, after much experimenting, the destroyer was provided with the means of combating this new menace.

Admiral Sir John Fisher, who became First Sea Lord in 1904, was very interested in all these new developments and, being a man of advanced ideas, he was determined that the Royal Navy should have up-to-date ships, including submarines and destroyers, and the best weapons and equipment available. Many naval officers laughed at the new submarines, which they called 'Fisher's toys'; as events proved, they were anything but a toy, but a method of attack that was to prove a major weapon in two world wars.

THE EXPANSION OF THE BRITISH EMPIRE

Meanwhile the British Empire was expanding widely. From an agricultural country with a population of seven millions at the time of Trafalgar, the Industrial Revolution had changed her into the greatest manufacturing country in the world by the end of the century, with a population of 32 millions to support. This meant that she could no longer grow sufficient food for her people. Her exports had to be sold abroad and food imported in exchange. New markets for British goods were found, and during the long reign of Queen Victoria new possessions and bases were added to the Empire – Cyprus, Ceylon, Aden, Singapore and Hong Kong, to mention only a few. Besides serving as trading posts, they provided 'coaling stations' for the Royal and Merchant Navies.

Admiral Fisher had the foresight to build up a navy capable of keeping the high seas open to our merchant shipping. He was a man of remarkable vision, and even forecast that oil would take the place of coal as fuel in warships. The government, too, showed wisdom when on his advice it purchased shares in the newly-formed Anglo-Persian Oil Company.

CHAPTER SEVEN

The First World War and the League of Nations

THE NEW ENEMY – GERMANY

The Industrial Revolution gave Great Britain a lead over the whole world in manufactured exports. But other countries were quick to learn from us and they in turn became prosperous. Germany in particular was very jealous of Britain. She had expanded, too, and had possessions across the seas, but her rulers knew that unless they could match the Royal Navy they could never hope to achieve the greatness of Britain. Already Germany had been at war with France and it was apparent to many thinking people that Germany was bent on world domination. She began the building of a fleet to match our own and Lord Fisher knew that he must keep a British fleet in the North Sea to be prepared for any mischief from Germany. This meant the removal of some of our best ships from our stations abroad, from China, America and the Mediterranean. But as we were on friendly terms with Japan, China, America and France, they promised to assist us in sharing the defence of these areas. Meanwhile in Germany preparations went ahead for building a High Seas Fleet which was to be a match for the Royal Navy.

Outbreak of War, 1914

So both Great Britain and Germany built up mighty fleets in rivalry of one another. Both possessed battleships firing improved types of shells, battle cruisers – not as heavily armed and protected as a battleship but much faster – cruisers, destroyers and submarines. As the Germans built one class of battleship firing a certain size of shell, so we replied with one that could fire a bigger shell. A notable example of this competition was the German *König*-Class battleship firing a 12-in. shell, which was followed immediately by our *Warspite*-Class firing a 15-in. shell. So this race went on, until on 4th August 1914, when the German armies invaded Belgium, Great Britain declared war on Germany. By that time, as far as capital ships were concerned, we had 29 battleships to Germany's 23 and 6 battle cruisers to her 5. As Germany had attacked France, we sent the British Army to assist the latter; at the same time we tried to ensure that the German High Seas Fleet should not succeed in getting out into the Atlantic, where it would imperil our Merchant Navy bringing vital supplies to Britain. To bar the German navy from the Atlantic, the Grand Fleet under Admiral Jellicoe was based at Scapa

Flow, with Admiral Sir David Beatty in command of a striking force of battle cruisers. The other entrance to the Atlantic – the Channel – was guarded by the Dover Patrol and by minefields, whilst destroyer and submarine forces were based at Harwich to keep watch on any movements of the German Fleet.

Battle of Heligoland, 28th August 1914

Commodore Roger Keyes, in command of the Harwich submarine force, had been exploring the German coastline off Heligoland and discovered that the enemy maintained a constant daily patrol of this area. It was planned, therefore, to bring the enemy to action off their own coastline. The destroyer force from Harwich, commanded by Commodore Reginald Tyrwhitt, pushed its way into the mine-infested waters of the Heligoland Bight, whilst at a discreet distance astern Admiral Beatty lay in wait with his battle cruiser squadron. The destroyer force delivered its attack on the German patrol vessels, and German light cruisers hastened to their rescue. This was just what he wanted: as our destroyers turned, there, to the consternation of the enemy, was Beatty with his powerful squadron! Immediately the German cruisers turned tail for home, but not before Admiral Beatty had sent three of them to the bottom, crippled three more and sunk one destroyer for good measure. This was a serious reverse for the German High Command, and for some months no German surface craft ventured from their home ports.

German Surface Raiders – the *Emden*

Before the outbreak of war Germany had several cruisers at sea in foreign waters. The largest force was Admiral Von Spee's squadron of cruisers, which began to prey on unprotected shipping along the China coast. One of his cruisers, the *Emden*, was given a lone hand and operated with some success against our merchant ships in the Bay of Bengal. For three months the Indian Ocean and Bay of Bengal were searched for the *Emden*, until she was found and destroyed by HMAS *Sydney* in the first victory to be won by the newly-formed Australian Navy. But Von Spee, with the heavy cruisers *Scharnhorst* and *Gneisenau*, together with three light cruisers, could not be found – they seemed to have disappeared into the blue.

Battle of Coronel, 1st November 1914

As mysteriously as Von Spee had vanished from the China seas so he reappeared, this time in South American waters. In that area, in the Falkland Isles, was Rear-Admiral Cradock, in command of a much smaller and less powerful force. At once the Admiralty despatched the battleship *Canopus* to strengthen Admiral Cradock's fleet, but this new addition proved to be so slow that she was unable to keep up with the rest of the British squadron. Flinging all caution to the winds, Cradock decided to seek out the enemy without the help of the battleship, for already Von Spee and his cruisers were creating havoc among merchant shipping. On 1st November 1914 Von Spee was found near Coronel, off the coast of Chile. Immediately the British admiral tried to close the range on the enemy, but Von Spee kept out of range until the evening. Then, as the setting sun silhouetted the British cruisers on the western horizon, Von Spee opened fire. The heavier German guns were too much for Admiral Cradock, and in less than an hour the waves had closed over two of his gallant cruisers; a third one escaped.

Battle of the Falkland Isles, 8th December 1914

The news of this disaster, the first British naval defeat for over a hundred years, shocked the public at home and throughout the Empire. The invincible British Navy had suffered a defeat! The Germans were jubilant – but not for long, for the Admiralty had already detached two speedy battle cruisers from home waters to avenge the defeat. It had been clear to our Intelligence Service that Von Spee would make full use of his advantage by attacking our base in the Falkland Isles. Speed on our part was thus essential. The refit which the two battle cruisers were undergoing was quickly finished on the orders of Admiral Fisher, then First Sea Lord; and with the greatest possible speed HMS *Inflexible* and *Invincible*, commanded by Admiral Sturdee, steamed 8000 miles in less than one month, arriving at the Falkland Isles on the afternoon of 7th December. The next day, while the British ships were coaling, Von Spee appeared; but, seeing the tripod masts of the British battle cruisers, he immediately turned his squadron of five ships about and made off. This time, however, the Royal Navy was not to be cheated. The coaling was suspended and the order 'General Chase' was given. Although Von Spee tried his utmost to elude his pursuers, he found it impossible, and as the guns of the battle cruisers spoke he realised that his end had come. Before the close of the day four out of the five ships in his squadron had been sent to the bottom. The British defeat at Coronel had been avenged in a most decisive way and the faith of Great Britain in the power of the Royal Navy was restored.

The cruiser *Dresden*, which escaped, and the few remaining German cruisers still in foreign waters did not survive long. Those that were not destroyed scuttled themselves rather than face destruction at the hands of the Royal Navy. Once again the seas were safe for the passage of our merchantmen bringing supplies to Britain and her Allies.

Battle of the Dogger Bank, 24th January 1915

The battle of the Falkland Isles made the enemy realise the power of the British Navy, and as the German High Seas Fleet was bottled up in the North Sea, they decided to make use of their own battle cruisers in raids on English east coast towns. Before the end of 1914 both Scarborough and Hartlepool were bombarded. The enemy described these towns as fortified fortresses containing important gun emplacements. This was completely untrue, and their shells simply killed defenceless citizens. Admiral Beatty with his battle cruisers tried to intercept the enemy as they scuttled homewards, but the prevailing bad weather favoured the Germans, who, as one British naval officer wrote, 'came out of one rainstorm and disappeared into another'.

Later, in January 1915, German battle cruisers attempted another east coast raid, but this time Admiral Beatty's battle cruisers, supported by the Harwich destroyer force, had put to sea to intercept the enemy, who was encountered in the vicinity of the Dogger Bank. When the enemy realised he was in the presence of a stronger force he made for home at full speed. Admiral Beatty, who, like Nelson before him, was made a Flag Officer at the age of 39, raced after the Germans and opened fire as soon as the enemy battle cruisers came within range. At ten miles distance the first hits were observed, but there was no slackening of speed. The Germans retaliated well, fighting as they made for home. Three of their ships concentrated their fire on Beatty's flagship, the *Lion*, and she received a hit which forced her to reduce speed. At this moment one of the three German battle cruisers was on fire and the *Blücher*, an armoured cruiser, was obviously badly damaged. To Beatty this presented great possibilities – the complete destruction of the enemy. He therefore hoisted Nelson's favourite signal, 'Engage the enemy more closely'. Unfortunately, this was misunderstood by the other British battle cruisers: they thought it meant they should concentrate on sinking the already crippled *Blücher* rather than pursue the rest of the squadron, and as a result the enemy escaped.

The Battle of Jutland, 31st May 1916

The Dogger Bank action, incomplete as it was, put an end for some time to the appearance of German surface craft in the North Sea. But German naval architects had been very busy. As a result of the heavy damage incurred by their battle cruisers they made several improvements in the armour and magazine flooding arrangements of their vessels, and this was to prove of great importance in the next battle. Admiral Scheer became Commander-in-Chief of the German fleet at the beginning of 1916. He had been greatly impressed by the previous raids on the east coast of England, for he saw in them a means of destroying the British force of battle cruisers. His plans was that a force of battle cruisers should show themselves to the British Grand Fleet of the Norwegian coast and, knowing that the British battle cruisers would give chase, they were to be led into a trap just off the coast of Jutland, where the entire German High Seas Fleet would be lying in wait. Further, German U-boats were to assemble outside the British base at Scapa, where they would torpedo Admiral Jellicoe's capital ships as they raced out of harbour. To make certain of the whole picture as it progressed, zeppelins were to provide air reconnaissance.

By means of a new device, the hydrophone, our coastal craft detected the presence of this unusual number of U-boats, and Admiral Jellicoe thus realised that something was afoot and got his entire fleet to sea without the knowledge of the enemy. The situation became further complicated because of the weather, for low visibility prevented the German airships from carrying out their air survey. Because of this, Admiral Scheer, lying in wait off Jutland, had no idea of the size of the fleet he was to fight. The German Admiral Hipper, who was to show his battle cruisers as bait to the British Grand Fleet, was steaming northwards for this purpose, with the German High Seas Fleet 40 miles astern. To Hipper's amazement he sighted Admiral Beatty with a superior force of battle cruisers at sea. Immediately the German battle cruiser turned southwards to join their main fleet, and Beatty followed – into the trap. In a very short time Beatty secured a hit on one of the enemy ships, which burst into flames, but two of his own battle cruisers were hit in the magazine and blew up. Undaunted, Beatty carried on, when suddenly the German High Seas Fleet came in sight, steaming northwards. It was now Beatty's turn to alter course and get away from this prepared trap, and Admiral Scheer's moment for action as he ordered full speed ahead to the High Seas Fleet, now in pursuit of Beatty.

Every mile of this chase brought Admiral Scheer towards the British Grand Fleet steaming in great majesty towards the unsuspecting enemy. At about six in the evening the Germans found themselves opposed by the whole of Admiral Jellicoe's fleet. This was something that Scheer had not expected, and so began one of the most complicated battles in naval history. The trouble was the very poor visibility, which made it impossible to know at any one moment the exact position of any ship, and considering that over 250 warships on both sides were engaged in this action, it is easy to understand the confusion. The British battleships opened fire as Admiral Scheer did all he could to get out of this complicated trap, and great credit must be given to the German admiral for the manner in which he prevented the annihilation of his fleet. As he gave orders for evasive action, he sent his destroyers to the rear of his fleet, where, by means of smoke screens and torpedo attacks, they covered up the withdrawal of their capital ships. The smoke screens only added to the very poor visibility, and as dusk fell the German fleet, though badly mauled, managed to hide itself in the gloom. Radar was, of course, unknown during the First World War and night actions were thus very difficult. But Scheer had to get home somehow and Jellicoe was determined to prevent this if he could. There were only three avenues of escape for the German fleet to their naval bases. Two of these were barred by Admiral Jellicoe's fleet, whilst the third had been made very unhealthy by a minefield hastily laid by one of the British minelayers.

Admiral Scheer, with the luck of a gambler, chose the easiest path – through the minefield – and managed to get his fleet past this barrier with the loss of only one battleship. Many of our destroyers made contact with the enemy during darkness and gallantly threw themselves at Scheer's fleet in an attempt to prevent its escape. Their sacrifices were in vain, for Scheer managed to reach port, where he immediately announced a great German victory! Our losses (three battle cruisers, three cruisers and eight destroyers) certainly appeared heavy – in fact, they were greater than those of the enemy – but there is really no doubt that Jutland was a British strategical victory, for the enemy withdrew from the battle area and – what is more important – they never effectively put to sea again during the war.

During the battle of Jutland a St. Vincent boy, Jack Cornwell, was one of a gun's crew aboard HMS *Chester*. When the *Chester* was under fire, though the rest of the gun's crew were killed or wounded and he himself was seriously wounded, Boy Cornwell continued to lay and fire the gun until he collapsed and died. For his supreme courage and devotion to duty he was awarded the Victoria Cross.

THE U-BOAT CAMPAIGN

The enemy started to use his U-boats in 1915, but when the passenger liner *Lusitania* was sent to the bottom in May of that year with a great loss of American lives the diplomatic protests of the United States were strong enough to persuade Germany to call off this type of warfare. The land fighting in France was not progressing as well as the Germans had hoped, and one thing they did not wish was that the United States should join the war on the side of Britain and France. They were therefore very careful not to upset the Americans. Admiral Scheer, however, had different ideas. He knew that his surface fleet could not match the might of the Royal Navy – but U-boats in sufficient numbers could destroy British merchantmen and so cripple Britain. This argument appealed to the German High Command, who gave orders for the construction of a large U-boat fleet.

By February 1917 this fleet was in action, to deadly effect. Without any respect for International Law, the U-boats sank ships of any nationality at sight. This threat to our supplies had become serious by April, when one out of every four ships entering or leaving English ports was sunk by this inhumane warfare. We replied by arming some of our merchant ships with medium guns, which were hidden by screens until the moment when the ship was challenged by a U-boat. Then the screens were dropped, and one salvo was sometimes enough to blast the U-boat out of the water. Such ships were known as 'Q-ships', or 'Query ships'. Unfortunately, they had the effect after a while of forcing the U-boats to attack whilst submerged, which only made the problem worse from our viewpoint. To strike a blow at the very heart of U-boat activity, Admiral Sir Roger Keyes, on 23rd April (St. George's day) 1918, made a daring raid on Zeebrugge, one of the harbours in Belgium whence U-boats came out into the North Sea. The canal at Zeebrugge was put temporarily out of action for less than 24 hours, but the enemy's main base for his ocean-going U-boats was farther to the eastward and was not affected by this raid.

The situation at home became increasingly difficult. Food was very scarce and rationing had to be imposed. But despite the use of new methods of defence, Q-ships, the depth-charge (a wartime invention) and the use of hydrophones, British merchant shipping losses grew at an alarming rate – until we brought in the convoy system. Then, with improvements in the types of depth-charges used by the convoy escorts, our losses began to fall. By this time the United States had entered the war on our side, and by the end of the year we were able to transport thousands of American soldiers across the Atlantic without loss. The arrival of these fresh troops at the front was too much for the enemy, and in October 1918, when the German High Seas Fleet was ordered to put to sea for one last effort, the order led to mutiny. Soon Germany could stand no more and asked for an armistice, which was signed on 11th November 1918. A week after the armistice a fleet of 70 German warships sailed into British ports for internment. But this humiliation was more than the proud Imperial German Navy could stand; and in the summer of 1919, as a protest against the Peace Treaty of Versailles, all German heavy ships in British ports were scuttled by their own officers.

BETWEEN THE TWO WORLD WARS

The Treaty of Versailles had good intentions, but not all its decisions were wise. Quite rightly, Germany was forbidden to maintain a navy or manufacture armaments, but as she was given very little opportunity for trade she had less money to pay her debts. The men who attempted to punish Germany attempted also to build a safer world. They hoped that this could be done by means of the League of Nations, which came into being in 1920. Although this brotherhood of nations was the idea of President Wilson, it was not popular generally in America and the United States refused to become a member.

The war had been a great strain on Great Britain and had cost the country a lot of money. America and Japan, however, both of whom were our allies during the war, came out of it far better than we did, for neither of those countries was actively engaged in the whole of the war. Various conferences were held between the United Kingdom and her wartime allies in an attempt to define the size of their respective navies. These showed that Great Britain could no longer hope to have the largest navy in the world, but would have to accept one equal in size to America's. At home this step appealed to public opinion, for the general outcry was 'disarmament'. This wish was reflected in the amount of money voted annually by Parliament for the navy – the sum in question becoming less and less each year until 1932. We agreed to limit the size of our capital ships, but in general there was little agreement on other types of vessels. Japan was against the use of battleships, while America wanted them. We were against the use of submarines, but were opposed in this by Japan, Italy and France. Not much was said about aircraft carriers, for no one was quite sure what part they would play in a future war. During the First World War the Royal Naval Air Service had been formed and a few ships were fitted out as 'carriers'. These carried seaplanes which were fitted with wheels and which took off from ships but landed on the water. Later, deck landings were made, but these were very primitive: in the early stages, as the aircraft came into land its engines were throttled down while a party of sailors on the flight deck grabbed it in mid-air and pulled it down! Further experimenting led to the use of arrester gear, which made landing safer. By 1930 the Royal Navy had four aircraft carriers but no control over the aircraft aboard, which was the responsibility of the Air Ministry.

With this disagreement between nations over the type of navy they should have, and the uncertainty of all regarding the aircraft carrier, the nations concerned went their separate ways. This was perhaps just as well, for in Germany a new danger arose. The German leaders were disgusted with the terms of the Peace Treaty and for some years had been rearming in secret. In 1933 Adolf Hilter came to power; two years later he publicly denounced the Peace Treaty and proclaimed that Germany was rearming. The serious view that was taken of this announcement is shown by the amount of money spent on the Royal Navy about that time. In 1934 the figure was £56 million, but in 1935 £149 million. At last we had realized the renewed menace of Germany, which once again wished to enslave Europe and dominate the world. The outbreak of war was once more on the horizon. Our navy was greatly reduced in size; and although many new ships were ordered in 1936, a large proportion of the fleet was either uncompleted or had not been modernised when war actually broke out.

CHAPTER EIGHT

The Second World War and the United Nations

NAZI GERMANY'S AGGRESSION

Hitler was determined to reverse Germany's defeat in the First World War and from 1936 onwards he tried to show by menaces that Germany had the power to do this. He invaded Czechoslovakia in 1938, and then threatened Poland. As Great Britain was pledged to support Poland against German aggression she had no option but to declare war on Germany when the German armies overran that unhappy country on 3rd September 1939. For years before the war German factories had concentrated on the mass-production of tanks, aircraft, guns and army vehicles, but little money had been devoted to her navy. At first Hitler thought that if he did not challenge the Royal Navy Great Britain might allow him a free hand in Europe. With these hopes, he pinned his faith on his army and air force, both of which had been expanded. By comparison with the Royal Navy the German fleet was small: nevertheless at the outbreak of war it included two uncompleted battleships, three pocket battleships and a cruiser and destroyer force, as well as 57 submarines, although many of the latter were unfit for ocean service. Although it was not a formidable fleet, it was none the less quite a powerful one.

The Magnetic Mine

In the very first month of the war Hitler sprang his first surprise – the magnetic mine, which was a British invention of the First World War. These were parachuted from aircraft in the shallow waters off the east coast. Within two months so many ships had been sunk that sailings from the Thames were stopped. HMS *Gipsy*, a destroyer, was blown in half by an air-laid mine at Harwich harbour, and many Dutch liners met the same fate in the shallows off Felixstowe[1]: but the secrets of this dreadful device were soon revealed when a magnetic mine was found

[1] Before the boys of HMS *Ganges* at Shotley Nr Ipswich, were moved to the Isle of Man, they did valuable work in assisting with the many casualties that were brought into *Ganges*. At one period so many bodies were brought ashore that the laundry within the establishment had to be used as a mortuary. Many of these were buried at Shotley Church, where the inscriptions on the gravestones tell their own stories of the terrible destruction produced by the magnetic mine. The boy entry has now ceased and *Ganges* has closed.

intact. At great risk to their lives, officers and men of HMS *Vernon*[1] took it to pieces and unveiled the secrets of its mechanism. Steps were then taken to protect ships from the mine by an electrical process called 'degaussing'. New methods of minesweeping were devised. By the beginning of 1940 the menace of the magnetic mine had been overcome, but not before it had claimed eighty merchant ships as its victims.

Early U-Boat Activity

Although Germany's U-boat force was very small during the first year of the war, and only six or seven of them were at sea at any one time, they took a heavy toll of our shipping. On the very first day of the war the liner *Athenia* was sunk by a U-boat without warning. The aircraft carrier HMS *Courageous* sank in three minutes after a U-boat attack off the south-west of Ireland, while the battleship HMS *Royal Oak* was torpedoed in harbour at Scapa Flow. This daring feat shocked the Royal Navy, for some of the entrances to the harbour were supposed to be protected against the entry of U-boats by sunken block-ships. But by brilliant seamanship the U-boat commander edged his craft through a gap between the block-ships, fired his torpedoes at the *Royal Oak* and, during the ensuing commotion, retraced his track to the comparative safety of the open sea.

Merchant shipping, too, suffered greatly: 164 ships were sent to the bottom in the first six months of war – and this was achieved by a mere handful of U-boats!

German Surface Raiders

Two German 'pocket battleships', the *Admiral Graf Spee* and the *Deutschland*, were at sea when war broke out. These miniature battleships were fast and carried six 11-inch guns and a secondary armament of eight 5.9-inch guns. Also at sea were the two more powerful German battle cruisers, *Scharnhorst* and *Gneisenau* – in all, a really powerful force to prey on our merchant shipping, but, surprisingly, they did very little damage. On 24th November 1939 the armed merchant cruiser, *Rawalpindi*, on patrol off Iceland, sighted the battle cruiser *Scharnhorst*. Although the *Rawalpindi* could only bring to bear a broadside of four 6-inch guns against the *Scharnhorst*, she attacked the warship and fought on until all her guns' crews had been killed and their guns put out of action. Ablaze from stem to stern, she sank with the loss of all but 38 of her crew. This gallant action roused the Home Fleet; but the *Scharnhorst*, in company with the *Gneisenau*, knowing their positions had been revealed, retired at full speed for Germany.

The Battle of the River Plate, 13th December 1939

As for the pocket battleships – the *Deutschland* sank only two merchant ships before returning to Germany in November 1939; her sister ship

[1] HMS Vernon is a naval training school at Portsmouth.

the *Graf Spee* operated in the South Atlantic and the Indian Ocean, where she played a lone hand in her attacks on shipping. By 13th December 1939 she had sent nine merchant ships to the bottom, when she met HM cruisers *Ajax, Achilles* (of the Royal New Zealand Navy) and *Exeter*. The *Ajax* and *Achilles* had 6-inch guns and the *Exeter* 8-inch, but one broadside of the *Graf Spee's* guns was more powerful than all the cruisers' guns combined. The only advantage held by Commodore Harwood, who was in command of the squadron, was a superiority in speed. He could afford to spread his ships and allow them to attack the *Graf Spee* separately, in the hopes that the raider would concentrate her fire on one ship. This is just what happened, for HMS *Exeter* bore the full weight of the 11-inch shells from the *Graf Spee* for a full twenty minutes until, because of flooding, she was unable to fire a single gun. The 11-inch guns were then turned on the *Ajax* and *Achilles*, but by skilful handling both avoided serious damage and the *Graf Spee* was herself damaged by shells. Aided by a smoke screen she made off, and a running engagement followed in which four of the guns of the *Ajax* were rendered useless by an 11-inch shell from the *Graf Spee*. With two ships now seriously damaged, Commodore Harwood kept within shadowing distance of the enemy, who made for the neutral harbour of Montevideo. For the next four days the three cruisers, reinforced by HMS *Cumberland*, patrolled the wide estuary of the River Plate, waiting for the *Graf Spee* to reappear. When at last the pocket battleship emerged, on 17th December, she blew herself up. For several months the German menace was lifted from the South Atlantic.

THE NORWEGIAN CAMPAIGN

Early in April 1940 Hitler launched a lightning invasion of Norway, with the help of his powerful air force. Although British and French naval forces were taking part in minelaying operations near the Norwegian coast, the Germans managed to land their troops by surprise. The British destroyer HMS *Glowworm*, of some 1300 tons, had been covering the minelaying operation and in very bad weather was searching for a man she had lost overboard. In this search, Lieut.-Commander Roope, the Commanding Officer, lost touch with the main naval force and was suddenly attacked by a German destroyer. Then another appeared, and in raging seas – when two men were hurled overboard – the *Glowworm* made off, with the enemy in pursuit. Then came a brief respite, for the enemy gave up the chase. But Lieut.-Commander Roope was determined to discover what the enemy was doing, so he turned and followed the German destroyers, only to find himself facing the 10 000-ton German cruiser *Admiral Hipper*. Roope knew he had no earthly chance of survival, for what could his four 4.7-inch guns do against the *Admiral Hipper's* eight 8-inch? And so he resolved to inflict as much damage as possible on the enemy before being sunk. Long before the *Glowworm's* guns were within range, she was hit mercilessly by the heavy shells from the *Admiral Hipper*. But the *Glowworm* was game. She zigzagged, made smoke screens and fired torpedoes at the enemy – but the struggle was a hopeless one. Then Lieut.-Commander Roope decided to ram the *Admiral Hipper*, and, under terrific fire from all the German guns, the bows of the *Glowworm* crumpled against the side of the cruiser, which was badly damaged. In this terrific inferno of flame and smoke the destroyer broke away, still with her guns firing, and Lieut.-Commander Roope gave the order to abandon ship. The action was over and the German cruiser lowered a boat to pick up survivors – but the gallant Commander and 117 of his comrades perished, and only 31 of the ship's complement escaped with their lives. For this most courageous action against the enemy, Lieut.-Commander Roope received the posthumous award of the Victoria Cross.

The Struggle for Narvik, April 1940

Although the German landings had been successful, the British Government hoped to recapture two of the important Norwegian ports, Narvik and Trondheim. In the first battle of Narvik, in atrocious weather, a brilliant action was fought against both German ships and shore batteries. Our submarines, too, made daring attacks on enemy shipping bringing supplies to the German troops. We managed to land our own soldiers, but as the main ports were in enemy hands we were forced to use smaller and less useful ones. But we sadly lacked aircraft, while the enemy had plenty – and full control of all Norwegian airfields. A few days later the second battle of Narvik took place, in which 'Tribal' Class destroyers, assisted by the battleship HMS *Warspite* (of First World War fame), destroyed the enemy destroyers and shipping in the fjord. But in the end the enemy air superiority began to tell and it was decided to evacuate our troops, as well as the King of Norway and many of his countrymen who wished to take up the fight against Germany as the Free Norwegian Forces.

DUNKIRK, 1940

Our failure in the Norwegian campaign led to a change in the Government: Mr. Winston Churchill took over as Prime Minister from Mr. Neville Chamberlain. On the very day he assumed responsibility (10th May) German troops invaded Holland and Belgium. Six days later their lightning attacks, which were preceded by intensive bombing, forced these countries to surrender. By the end of May German mechanised forces had broken through the Allied lines and reached Boulogne and Ostend, thus pinning down the British Expeditionary Force and other Allied forces in the area around Dunkirk. This was a situation which called for the Navy's immediate assistance in the form of mass evacuation. Forty-one destroyers, over 200 smaller naval craft and hundreds of small boats – in fact, anything that could float – were used for this stupendous task. At the height of the emergency, when time meant so much, one diesel lighter, which had lain on the Sheerness mud for ten years, could not be started. The manager of the firm which had built its engines was roused from his bed at 2 a.m. With a group of mechanics he was rushed to the lighter and before dawn it, too, was on its way to Dunkirk.

While the Royal Air Force was doing a magnificent job in bombing enemy airfields behind the lines and engaging his aircraft in the air, thousands of men waded out to the hundreds of ships and small craft waiting to take them home. A shuttle service ran from Dunkirk to British ports. In spite of continual interference by German aircraft, which flew over the ships and beaches bombing and machine-gunning our soldiers, about 224 000 British and 114 000 French troops were brought safely to Britain, a total of 338 000 men; of these, about 309 000 were conveyed in British vessels and the rest in Allied vessels. In addition, 27 936 men were evacuated, for the most part in British vessels, during the few days before Operation 'Dynamo' (the code name for the evacuation) began.

Anxious Days

Most of the rescued French troops planned to continue the fight against Germany under the name of 'Free French Forces', as their own government in France had accepted the German peace terms. In Britain, besides this large French force, were many smaller forces of various nationalities, all of whom were determined to carry on the war against Hitler. Mussolini, the Dictator of Italy, thinking that Germany was winning, now decided to declare war on Britain and become Hitler's ally. This did not worry us unduly, because there was some doubt about the Italian navy's fighting qualities; but as their fleet was both modern and fast and included many submarines, it was capable of providing the Royal Navy with quite a difficult task in the Mediterranean. What immediately concerned the Admiralty, however, was the French warships in English ports at the time of Dunkirk. Already we had some Polish destroyers serving with the Navy. But with the French the situation was different; as their government had surrendered to the enemy, many of the French ships might wish to return home and give up the struggle. To prevent this happening, French ships in British waters were boarded by the Navy and taken over. The French crews did not resist, except the crew of the giant French submarine *Surcouf*, when two RN officers and a rating and a French officer were killed. Later, this submarine played an important part in convoy work. As she carried two 8-inch guns as well as a seaplane, she proved a useful convoy escort.

It was a difficult time for our Free French allies because the new French government, with its headquarters at Vichy, was openly in favour of the German occupation. But gradually, through the years that followed, Resistance groups were formed against the Germans, and when the Allied landings took place these groups proved a great help to the liberating armies.

Hitler's Plans to Invade Great Britain

These were dark days for Britain – our armies had been forced out of France, the Germans were in control of all ports from the north of Norway right down to the Franco-Spanish border, and Hitler was intent on bringing Britain to her knees. Britain's aircraft factories, however, had been working at full pressure and a mighty force of Spitfire and Hurricane fighters was ready, not to mention the rapidly-mounting bomber force. These bombers, together with naval vessels, carried out persistent attacks on the French Channel ports where it was known that transport barges were being assembled for an invasion. Heavy air raids were directed by the enemy at south-east England in an attempt to gain air supremacy, but in the Battle of Britain our fighters shot the German Luftwaffe out of the skies and forced Hitler to abandon his invasion plan. Even if this had failed and Hitler had gained freedom of the skies, it is difficult to imagine how he could have transported his troops to England with the Royal Navy between them and the English coast. Both France and Spain had attempted it in the past and failed.

THE MEDITERRANEAN CAMPAIGN

His plans to invade England having been foiled, Hitler increased the number of his U-boats with the intention of starving Britain out of existence; and at the same time he intensified the air raids on London and industrial centres throughout the United Kingdom. But already his new ally Italy was causing him concern in the Mediterranean. Libya, in North Africa, had been colonised by the Italians before the war and, as the Italians were now our enemies, British land forces from our bases in Egypt had attacked and defeated Italian troops in Libya. In addition, the Italian fleet, snug in harbour at Taranto, was surprised by Swordfish aircraft from HMS *Illustrious*. These aircraft – 'Stringbags', as they were called – secured hits with their torpedoes on three battleships and two cruisers.

These setbacks came as an unwelcome surprise to Mussolini, who had inflated ideas of reviving the old Roman Empire and who already had joined Hitler in the war because he thought that Germany was winning. To further his ambitions Mussolini sent his troops to invade Greece; but, as in Libya, they too met determined opposition. Threatened, therefore, with being driven out of Libya by British forces and finding that his Greek campaign was held up by stout Greek resistance, Mussolini appealed to his partner in crime, Hitler, for assistance. Very soon experienced German forces invaded Greece and began to reinforce the Italian troops in Libya. For this purpose, they had to cross from Italy to Libya in Italian ships escorted by the Italian navy, which was far bigger than our own Mediterranean Fleet and contained some very modern and extremely fast vessels. Our warships had the greatest difficulty in bringing them to action, for on frequent occasions the faster Italian ships were able to keep out of range. However, our submariners in the Mediterranean were only too delighted to show their skill and daring in attacks against Italian shipping. We have all great cause to remember the German U-boats, but perhaps few of us realise the high standard of skill of our own submarine commanders.

The German U-boats and their crews were 'mass-produced' for the sole purpose of sinking slow-moving merchant ships. They had no success against our fast ships, and because of this the passenger liner *Queen Mary* and many vessels like her were able to transport troops across the oceans in safety and without escorts. The Italians, who had many fast liners, copied this idea, but with different results, for our submarines, whose crews were more highly trained, sank five of their fastest liners, each of about 17 000 tons, within the space of three months.

Lieut.-Commander Wanklyn

Perhaps the greatest of our submariners was Lieut.-Commander David Wanklyn, VC, DSO and two bars. He commanded HM S/M *Upholder*, one of the small submarines of the 'U' class (650 tons). There were five submarines of this class based on Malta and charged with the task of preventing German troops and supplies from reaching Libya. Wanklyn quickly showed his daring and skill by sinking many large supply ships, and even their escorts. He had been awarded the DSO for his success in submarine patrols.

After one such success his submarine was seen by Italian destroyers and he was forced to dive deep to avoid their depth charges. Only a few hours previously he had done the same thing and his asdic set had been put out of action by depth charges. This meant that the submarine was 'deaf' when submerged, for an asdic set gives timely warning of enemy movements. Without it the only warning is the noise heard by the human ear; when this happens it is usually too close for comfort. By skilful handling he managed to survive this second depth-charge attack, and when all was quiet he brought the *Upholder* up to periscope depth. As he was due to return to Malta for more torpedoes (he had but two left) he had a last look round before altering course. In the glow of the sunset he sighted three large liners racing along at top speed and, as far as he could tell through the periscope, they were escorted by five destroyers.

Although he had but two torpedoes and was without the use of his asdic set, this was an opportunity that Wanklyn could not resist. As it was now dusk, he dared not attack on the surface with five enemy destroyers about, so he manœuvred the *Upholder* by viewing the scene through the eye of the periscope – a difficult feat in the fast-fading light. He put his submarine right amidst the enemy, raised his periscope and saw the transports – but not the escorts. Seizing this opportunity, he sent his two torpedoes on their way, and almost at the same moment the periscope revealed a huge black V heading straight for him – the bows of a destroyer! As he was crash-diving, the thirty-three members of the *Upholder's* crew distinctly heard the explosions as the two torpedoes found their mark. But within three minutes the *Upholder* herself became the hunted as the crash of depth charges – two a minute – exploded round the hull, close enough to smash the electric light bulbs. Thirty-three depth charges exploded near enough to make things very uncomfortable – and all within twenty minutes. And then came the unmistakable beat of the propellers of one of the escorts. Louder and louder they became till they were churning the water directly overhead and then came an ear-splitting crash as four more charges exploded so close as to lift the submarine bodily in the water. But the rivets held, the enemy passed by and David Wanklyn was able to surface, where he saw oil and wreckage from the liner he had sunk. It turned out to be the *Conte Rosso*, a 17 800-ton transport. For this action, he was awarded the VC and many of his crew were decorated. His work continued and before his last patrol he had sunk 97 000-tons of merchant shipping, one destroyer and three enemy U-boats! Just before the *Upholder* was due to return home she was lost together with her brilliant CO and all her crew, while attacking a heavily-escorted Italian convoy. Because of the courageous and determined attacks by our submarines one half of the men, munitions and fuel which the enemy attempted to transport to Africa were sunk on the way.

German Air Attacks in the Mediterranean

With Italy now Germany's ally, many new airfields were made available to the German air force, in particular in Sicily. From there the Germans kept up persistent attacks on our base at Malta, and by dive-bombing tactics they made convoying to Malta a very dangerous job. In January 1941 fifty-eight raids were made by the German air force on Malta, and our convoys bringing supplies to the base suffered as well. The cruiser *Southampton* was sunk and heavy damage was incurred by the carrier *Illustrious*. Because of the great superiority of the German air force –

The Armada off Fowey: the English Fleet chasing the Spaniards up the Channel

Battle of Texel, 1673, during the Third Dutch War

Battle of the Saintes 9 April 1782: Admiral Rodney after a long chase and running fight defeated a large French fleet on its way to invade the British possession of Jamaica

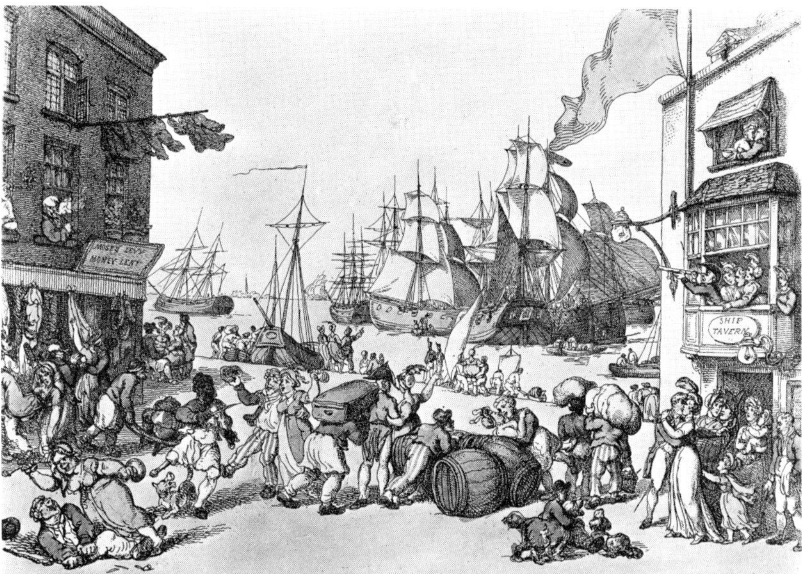

Portsmouth Point during the time of the Napoleonic Wars

Battle of the Nile, 1 August 1798. The French flagship *L'Orient* was blown up during the action and Nelson gained a crushing victory leaving Napoleon and his army isolated in Egypt

Gun-deck of a 1st rate of Nelson's day

Hoisting Nelson's famous signal 'England expects that every man will do his duty'

A burial at sea

HMS *Warrior*, launched in 1860, the first British warship with an all-metal hull. She was propelled by both sail and steam. She is still afloat today and it is hoped to restore the vessel and to exhibit her in Portsmouth

HMS *Devastation*, built in 1873, the first really modern battleship. Propelled entirely by steam, she carried 25 ton guns in revolving turrets

Admiral Sir John Fisher on board HMS *Renown*. A man of dynamic personality, exceptional determination and foresight. Lord Fisher (as he became in 1909) played a major role in creating a powerful Navy in the years preceding the First World War and as First Sea Lord, he directed it with boldness and skill. He died in 1920

Admiral Beatty on the bridge

A British sea-plane of the First World War. The pilot has just released a pigeon carrying a message. Early sea-planes landed on the sea and were hoisted inboard

The *Admiral Graf Spee* in flames off Montivideo

HMS *Warspite*, famous 15-inch gun battleship of the First World War was destined to play an important part in the Second World War. She fought at the Battle of Narvik in 1940 and bombarded the Italian mainland in 1943

General de Gaulle, head of the Free French Forces, visiting the submarine *Surcouf*. This submarine was in 1940, the largest in the world. She had a complement of 150, carried twin 8-inch guns and a small sea-plane. After Dunkirk she frequently acted in convoys as an escort but in April 1942, she was reported missing

Our war time leaders. From left to right: Sir Charles Portal (Chief of Air Staff), Sir Alan Brooke (Chief of the Imperial General Staff), Winston Churchill (Prime Minister) and Sir Andrew Cunningham (First Sea Lord and Chief of Naval Staff)

Lt-Commander Malcolm Wanklyn and officers of HM Submarine *Upholder*

The chariot – a small assault craft designed to travel both on and below the surface. The two-man crew, suitably attired, sat astride. Each chariot, carried an explosive charge which could be attached to the target-ship below the waterline

A British 'midget' submarine of the type which attacked the German 15-inch gun battleship *Tirpitz* in Alten fiord, Norway in September, 1943

The American General, Douglas MacArthur reading the surrender terms to the Japanese on board USS *Missouri* in Tokyo Bay, 14 August 1945

Suez Crisis 1956. Troops being ferried ashore in landing craft and helicopters

Commandos landing by helicopter, ready for immediate action

An assault party of Royal Marines leaving HMS *Nubian* in *Gemini* raiding craft for a beach landing exercise

HM Submarine *Courageous* – one of the *Fleet* or – *Valiant* class

The 12 000 ton Assault ship HMS *Intrepid* which operates a flight of helicopters and is armed with Seacat missiles and two 40 mm Bofors guns

HMS *Invincible*. An anti-submarine carrier, launched in 1977 and first commissioned in July 1980 in the presence of HM the Queen and HRH Prince Philip. She carries Sea Harrier V/STOL aircraft and Sea King Helicopters

HMS *Glamorgan*. One of the *County* class guided missile destroyers of over 5000 tons displacement

HMS *Ardent* – one of the *Amazon* class of frigates (type 21). Completed in 1977, she has a complement of about 170

The gas-turbined propelled frigate HMS *Broadsword*. An all-metric warship and the first to be built around an all-missile armament

Malta at one period had only three aircraft[1] – a great deal of the much-needed supplies was brought to Malta by the bigger types of submarine. Petrol, stores, torpedoes for our submarines – all were carried under water, so great was the menace of the Luftwaffe. But it must be emphasised that the danger came chiefly from the German air force and not from the Italian navy.

The Battle of Cape Matapan, March 1941

The Commander-in-Chief, Mediterranean (Admiral Sir Andrew Cunningham), who had a part of his fleet based on Gibraltar and the remainder on Alexandria, tried many times to bring the Italian navy to action. Towards the end of March 1941 a force comprising a battleship and several cruisers and destroyers was shadowed by our Eastern Mediterranean fleet. The aircraft carrier HMS *Formidable* was in company and her aircraft managed to damage the battleship, some 60 miles ahead of our own capital ships. By this time the enemy was making full speed for home and Admiral Cunningham could not hope to overtake him before dark. In further attacks by carrier-borne aircraft the Italian 8-inch cruiser *Pola* was torpedoed. As darkness fell the Italians were just off Cape Matapan, and southernmost point of Greece. Two of their cruisers, which had been despatched to look for the *Pola*, ran into our battleships. In a matter of seconds they were blown out of the water, together with one destroyer. This action – in which our total loss was one aircraft – had the effect of keeping the rest of the Italian fleet in harbour for many months.

The Hunting of the *Bismarck*

Just about this time, in the Atlantic, the Germans decided to send their recently completed battleship *Bismarck* and cruiser *Prinz Eugen* to prey on our convoys. The warships were spotted by two of our cruisers north of Iceland on 23rd May, and the following day our own battleship HMS *Prince of Wales* and the handsome-looking battle cruiser HMS *Hood* engaged them. Unfortunately, the *Hood* was hit by a shell which blew up her magazine, and she sank within three minutes. Only three survived out of her crew of nearly 1500. The *Prince of Wales* had been damaged too, but the *Bismarck* had also been hit and she made off, shadowed by two of our cruisers. Contact was lost until the morning of 26th May, when the *Bismarck* was sighted on a westerly course by an aircraft of Coastal Command. There was no sign of the *Prinz Eugen*, apparently, with her superior speed, she had parted company and made for home – actually to Brest. It seemed probable that the *Bismarck* would make for Brest, and the German air force was warned so that it could give her protection as soon as she came within flying range. Every Royal Naval

[1] Ancient Gladiators nicknamed 'Faith', 'Hope', and 'Charity'.

vessel within striking distance was warned to prevent her escaping. Aircraft from HMS *Victorious* fought their way through biting head winds, heavy rain and low cloud to deliver their torpedo attacks under ferocious fire from the *Bismarck*. Aircraft from the carrier HMS *Ark Royal* also obtained hits on the *Bismarck* which slowed her down and considerably damaged her steering. Her guns however were still intact, but on the morning of 27th May the battleships HMS *King George V* and *Rodney* silenced them, before torpedoes from the cruiser HMS *Dorsetshire* at last sank her. The *Bismarck* was the last heavy surface warship raider to attempt attacks on our shipping in the Atlantic. After her loss the Germans stepped up the production of their U-boats for the Battle of the Atlantic.

Admiral Sir Philip Vian and the Malta Convoys

Meanwhile, in the Mediterranean the German air force intensified its attacks on Malta; even our submarines bringing petrol to the island were forced to submerge during much of their time in harbour. But Malta fought on, although her supplies of food and ammunition were dangerously low. One small convoy got through to the island from Alexandria in January 1942, but in the following month another small west-bound convoy was forced to turn back because of the deadly attacks of German dive-bombers. In June, also, a larger west-going convoy was likewise obliged to turn back. By March the situation in Malta had become desperate. Supplies of food and ammunition were so low that it seemed as though surrender would only be a matter of time. That the gallant defence of the island against the Luftwaffe should cease through lack of supplies was unthinkable. It was imperative that a convoy should get through, and Admiral Sir Philip Vian, whose force was based on Alexandria, was ordered to make sure that it did.

Towards the end of March four merchant ships, together with Admiral Vian's escorting force of four cruisers and six destroyers, left Alexandria and shaped course for Malta. As eyes scanned the skies for enemy aircraft, not one man in that convoy had any doubts about what was expected. But, unexpectedly, enemy activity was to come first from another quarter – the Italian navy.

Since the battle of Cape Matapan, just one year previously, the Italian fleet had not ventured very far from its own harbours, but now, as Admiral Vian steamed towards Malta, he encountered a squadron of the Italian fleet, including a battleship and six cruisers, in the open seas and right in the path of Admiral Vian's convoy!

So it was something of a surprise when the lookouts reported the presence of this superior enemy force. This news, however, was the least of Admiral Vian's worries, and as the Italians tried to intercept the convoy the British force replied with a series of attacks under a smoke-screen. The Italians did not press home their numerical advantage and the convoy continued its way – but not unmolested as soon as it came within the range of German aircraft. There was no question of sounding 'Action Stations', for it was action all the time as the convoy, snakelike, twisted this way and that in its efforts to avoid the bombs that whistled down from above. Two of the merchant ships were sunk by direct hits, but the other two, though heavily damaged were shepherded into Malta amid the cheers of the inhabitants.

But the Germans were not to be cheated of their prey, and while the ships were being hastily unloaded German dive-bombers screamed down on the dockyard area. Wave after wave of bombers hurled down their bombs, but although the dockyard itself was almost totally destroyed, the ships were unloaded and Malta received her precious supplies.

Petrol continued to be supplied to Malta by our submarines, and occasionally Spitfires, flown off the decks of aircraft carriers, succeeded in reaching the island. As the year 1942 progressed a trickle of merchant vessels managed to get through to Malta and thus maintain supplies. Towards the end of the year more aircraft were flown there from carriers, and this reinforcement of the island's fighter defence began to have its effect. Enemy air activity decreased and it became possible to send a cruiser squadron and two destroyer flotillas to join the submarine force already based there.

THE BATTLE OF THE ATLANTIC

By March 1941, the mass production of U-boats enabled the enemy to adopt a new type of attack – hunting in packs. Our defences against this method were weak, simply because of the lack of escort vessels and aircraft to protect our convoys. Many of our destroyers had been lost or damaged in Norway and at Dunkirk, and of those remaining at the beginning of 1941 only one-half were available for active service. Although at this stage America was not in the war, she was a friendly neutral and gave us facilities for repairing our ships in American ports. Fifty old American destroyers were also supplied by America in exchange for British bases and, despite their age, were put to good use in convoy work.

Iceland had been occupied by our forces and Hvalfiord, near Reykjavik, was used as repair base for our destroyers, by basing there some of our new destroyer depot ships. It was off Reykjavik, during 1941, that a U-boat was captured intact. She had been attacked on the surface by a Hudson aircraft of Coastal Command. The hydroplanes of the U-boat were damaged and she could not submerge. Destroyers alongside the depot ship HMS *Hecla*, in Hvalfiord, were hastily despatched to the spot. At first the U-boat crew refused to surrender, but a few bursts of 0.5-inch machine-gun fire across her conning tower soon changed their minds. The U-boat was taken in tow by Anti-submarine trawlers and brought alongside the depot ship. The crew, the majority of whom were under 25 years of age, were taken aboard as prisoners of war. They were very frightened and all thought they were to be shot. When, however, they realised that we treated our prisoners humanely they became very bold and claimed that Germany would win the war within a few months.

This U-boat was a beautiful submarine, brand-new and on her maiden voyage from Hamburg, with her original supplies of torpedoes still intact, and her capture revealed much valuable information to the Admiralty. Many curious shaped tins were found aboard the U-boat and these proved of great interest to HMS *Hecla's* ships company, for when opened, they revealed such delicacies as ham, veal, sausages, and even cream cakes. Senior naval officers were flown to Iceland to examine the U-boat, and as the whole operation had been referred to in signals by the code word 'Graph', she was renamed HM S/M *Graph* and, with a British crew, joined our own submarine service.

The Gallant Fight of the *Jervis Bay*

During this period of intense U-boat activity it became known that the German pocket battle ship *Admiral Scheer*, armed with six 11-inch and six 5.9-inch guns, had left the Baltic port of Gdynia and was at large in the Atlantic. As Captain Fegen, Commanding Officer of HMS *Jervis Bay*, looked at his calendar on the morning of 5th November 1941 it is probable that what chiefly worried him was the thought of U-boats. The *Jervis Bay*, an 18-year-old converted merchant liner carrying seven 6-inch guns, was the only real defence to a convoy of 38 ships carrying petrol and food to Britain. Just after tea on that memorable day the pocket battleship was sighted on the horizon and approaching at full speed towards the convoy. Immediately 'Action Stations' was sounded aboard the *Jarvis Bay* and the convoy was ordered to scatter. The *Admiral Scheer* opened fire on the convoy at a range of 9½ miles, but by making use of smoke-screens the convoy quickly scattered to avoid certain destruction – but not the *Jervis Bay*. Captain Fegen steamed straight towards the oncoming enemy to draw her fire and so allow the convoy to escape. Towards this almost-certain death Captain Fegen steered his ship. It was a one-sided fight and the *Admiral Scheer* soon out-ranged and crippled the *Jervis Bay* with her more powerful guns. Badly wounded, with his arm drenched in blood, Captain Fegen desperately tried to control his ship, but as another salvo straddled the liner he realised that there was no chance of saving the ship – or himself, for he had been mortally wounded. In his dying moments he gave the orders to abandon ship, and his gallant crew ceased firing and their attempts to quell the fires on board, and made their way to the boats.

So sank the *Jervis Bay* and with her Captain Fegen, who by his gallant action had delayed the *Admiral Scheer's* attack on the convoy by at least an hour. In fact, so effective had been Captain Fegen's delaying action that when at last the pocket battleship was able to turn her attention to the rest of the convoy, she managed to sink only six ships of the thirty-eight. Sixty-five of Captain Fegen's gallant crew survived, though many of them were badly wounded and their bodies numbed with the freezing waters of the Atlantic. The *Admiral Scheer*, cheated of her prey, made her way to the South Atlantic. For his gallantry Captain Fegen was posthumously awarded the VC. One of his brothers, also a naval officer, summed up his last action in these words: 'It was the end he would have wished'.

The United States Enters the War

With the small number of escort ships available for duty, U-boats hunting in packs could afford to lie outside the asdic screening range of our destroyers and then, when the convoy was a slow one of 4–6 knots, overtake it and pick off ship after ship. In the middle of 1941 the control of Coastal Command aircraft was handed to the Admiralty; and when long-range aircraft became available, U-boats were forced to move from the west coast of the British Isles, their happy hunting-ground, farther out into the Atlantic.

In December 1941 Japan, which had joined in the war on the side of Germany and Italy, attacked without warning the chief American naval base in the Pacific, at Pearl Harbour, an action which at once caused the United States to enter the war as Great Britain's ally. The German reaction was swift – they immediately concentrated their submarines off the American coast. In the six months that followed they sank 412 merchant ships and 130 tankers – two and a quarter million tons of shipping! (The Americans had not then fully adopted the convoy system.)

In the early days many American pleasure resorts, such as Miami in Florida, were not blacked-out and continued to illuminate their sea fronts with miles of neon signs. This was a paradise for U-boats, which found American ships easy targets when silhouetted against this bright background. But after such terrific losses convoys were started along the American coast; and, like the British, the Americans were forced to black-out their coastline. This caused a movement of U-boats back to the Atlantic once again, where the 'wolf packs' kept up intensive attacks on convoys day and night. In November 1942, 83 ships were sunk, while in the whole of that year nearly five and a half million tons of shipping were sent to the bottom. Moreover, although we sank many U-boats, the enemy was building new ones at a faster rate, and at the end of 1942 they had over 400 submarines in service. By then, however, the range of Allied aircraft from both sides of the Atlantic had increased, thus forcing the U-boats to operate in mid-Atlantic, out of their reach. This concentration of submarines in a comparatively small area simplified the task of locating them, even when they were submerged. As for the 'wolf pack' technique, the leader, on sighting a convoy, reported the fact by W/T and these signals could be detected. The pack could only form on the surface, and if sufficient escort vessels could be spared from a convoy the menace could be overcome.

As more and more escort ships became available this detachment from the convoy to hunt the U-boats to exhaustion showed quick results. The code word 'Raspberry' was chosen to give warning of an impending U-boat kill. Immediately all the escorts to the convoy would fire star shells to illuminate the water and force the submarines to submerge, and then they would be attacked with greatly improved depth-charges.

With these new methods and the use of aircraft from the escort ships and very long-range aircraft from shore, U-boat losses began to mount, and by May 1943, the Germans were forced to withdraw their submarines from mid-Atlantic. The spirit of the U-boat crews was gradually broken as their losses increased and they failed to press home their attacks.

The turning-point in the Battle of the Atlantic had been reached.

Escape of the *Scharnhorst, Gneisenau* and *Prinz Eugen*

The two German battle cruisers *Scharnhorst* and *Gneisenau* had taken part in the landings of German forces in Norway and then, for a brief spell, they attacked Atlantic convoys. In March 1941 they were located by the Royal Air Force at Brest, where they were the target for many attacks by the RAF. It thus became very unhealthy for them at Brest, and the German High Command decided to move them. The Royal Navy was prepared for this and had kept a constant watch on the port; but, as luck would have it, on the night of 11th February 1942 HM S/M *Sealion* withdrew from her watching position to recharge her batteries, and the German battle cruisers, together with the *Prinz Eugen*, chose that very night to make their escape. With a strong destroyer escort the German ships slipped out into the darkness and made for the English Channel, a German port and comparative safety.

At 10 o'clock the following morning the news of the escape was given to Lieut.-Commander Esmonde, DSO, at the Fleet Air Arm headquarters at Lee-on-Solent. He had received his decoration for his daring attack on the *Bismarck* while he was serving in the carrier HMS *Victorious*. Within a few minutes he led his squadron of six Swordfish into the skies. These comparatively slow aircraft, with a fighter escort, flew off towards Calais to meet a force of some 33 German ships escorting the three powerful German cruisers!

The enemy were taking no chances, for when dawn broke they provided a great fighter umbrella for their valuable ships. Suddenly this fighter force ripped through the Swordfishes' fighter screen. Lieut.-Cdr. Esmonde lost contact with his squadron, machine-gun fire spattered his fuselage, but he retained his balance and flew on. Miraculously the rest of his squadron dodged the fighters and followed, taking up a V formation behind their leader. Then the battle cruisers were spotted and Lieut.-Cdr. Esmonde led his squadron to an almost certain death. Before he could even launch his torpedoes, Esmonde's plane was blown to bits by the inferno of fire from all the ships. The rest of his squadron pressed home their attacks and one torpedo secured a hit, but it did little damage; and almost before the aircraft could turn away, they were all shot out of the sky by the guns of the battle cruisers, which made good their escape. Lieut.-Cdr. Esmonde received a posthumous VC for his gallant action, fruitless though it was.

THE CALL FOR A SECOND FRONT

The help required by Mussolini in the Mediterranean was quickly supplied by seasoned German forces. With massive air support they quickly overran Greece and forced us to withdraw our troops in an evacuation that had to be carried out at night, so deadly were the attacks of German planes. Over 50 000 soldiers had been taken off by the Royal Navy by the end of April 1941. It was the same story on the island of Crete, in the eastern Mediterranean. Our forces had occupied this island in October 1940; but, with Greek airfields now in German hands, the superiority in numbers of German planes proved too much for our soldiers in Crete, who were subjected to murderous air attacks. The enemy even attempted a seaborne invasion of the island, but the Royal Navy prevented them from landing. Nevertheless the German air force was so powerful that our warship losses became very serious, and when German paratroops were dropped on Crete it was decided at the end of May to evacuate our 17 000 soldiers from the island. Assisted by submarines, the Royal Navy rescued the survivors of Crete, besides carrying out offensive operations against enemy supply ships.

Farther afield, the Japanese were having rapid successes. The surprise attack on Pearl Harbour had temporarily disabled the American Pacific fleet, and three days later, in attempting to cover Singapore from Japanese attacks, we suffered the loss of the battleship HMS *Prince of Wales* and battle cruiser HMS *Repulse* in a lightning attack by torpedo-carrying Japanese planes in the Gulf of Siam.

It was the same story all the time – the superiority in numbers of enemy aircraft. We had to keep a strong air force at home to carry out raids on Germany and to prevent the invasion of our land. But as yet there were few planes to spare for overseas operations. This was not generally realised by the public, who were constantly under air attack from German bombers. It is not surprising, therefore, that many people in this country were calling for a 'Second Front' – that is, to go over to the offensive against the enemy.

By the spring of 1942 matters looked even worse. The Japanese had captured Singapore, and with the evacuation of Crete we had lost our last foothold in continental Europe. Hitler had attacked Russia, too, and the Russian armies were retreating.

Some boost to morale was needed, some daring escapade was required to inspire our people, and after consideration the Cabinet gave approval to a raid on the port of St. Nazaire, on the Biscay coast.

The Raid on St. Nazaire

A new German battleship, the *Tirpitz*, had appeared in Norwegian waters, and it was thought that if ever she got into the Atlantic she would use the port and dock at St. Nazaire. The plan approved by the Cabinet was that the seaward end of the caissons, some 167 ft long, 54 ft high and 35 ft thick, should be destroyed. If successful, this would also prevent U-boats from sheltering in the many 'pens' within the port. One of the fifty ex-American destroyers lent to us and renamed the *Campbeltown*, was to be used as an explosion ship. The attack by this ship, its bows crammed with time-fused explosives, took place in the early hours of 28th March 1942. This daring feat was carried out in the face of withering fire from German gun positions on either side of the dock gates, while at the same time Commando troops attacked in motor launches.

Three naval VCs were won that night, one of them by AB Savage, a pompom gun-layer on one of the motor gunboats. When his boat came under severe fire from a German gun position he silenced the gun with one burst from his pompom. Another gun, this time from a pillbox on shore, was again silenced by one burst from AB Savage, right through the slit of the pillbox. Although his gunboat was being hit almost continously and he had been mortally wounded, he kept his gun firing up to the last moment. The courage of this man in attacking so many German gun positions was a great inspiration to all our gunboats' crews. The delayed-action charges in the *Campbeltown* were successfully fired and, while a confusion of German soldiers were running about on top of the dock, the ship exploded with a mighty roar and the dock gate was breached. Out of 630 men who took part in this daring raid, 144 were killed and only 270 returned home, the remainder being taken prisoner.

THE TURN OF THE TIDE

The St. Nazaire raid and a daring seaborne raid on Dieppe, in which many Canadian troops took part, showed the British public that we were capable of going over to the offensive; this, of course, is what we had been preparing for during the difficult days.

By May 1942 the Vichy French-held island of Madagascar, on the eastern side of South Africa, had been occupied in order to safeguard our convoys carrying troops to Egypt by way of the Cape of Good Hope. Month by month, convoys, sometimes carrying as many as 50 000 troops, were taken by this route to build up our army in Egypt ready to drive the enemy out of North Africa.

By November 1942 the Allies were in a position to strike. Landings in North Africa – at Algiers, Oran and Casablanca – had been planned. Seven convoys of some 350 ships carried British forces and supplies to North Africa, whilst a force direct from the United States landed at Casablanca on 8th November. At the same time our armies in Egypt, so painstakingly built up, began their offensive to squeeze the enemy out of Africa.

Now our turn had come – at last we had the men and the aircraft. Softened up by the guns from HM ships and attacks by Allied aircraft, the enemy put up very little resistance to the landings. The Vichy French harbour of Casablanca presented a sorry sight. Several Vichy warships were sunk, though the fighting efficiency of their uncompleted battleship *Jean Bart*, which was heavily bombed by aircraft, was not seriously impaired. The Americans had done their work well: Casablanca was in Allied hands, and the enemy found themselves sandwiched between two Allied forces. The problem soon became what to do with the prisoners, for over a quarter of a million were captured within a few days. The whole operation had so taken the enemy by surprise that during the actual landings not one ship was lost by U-boat activity.

Our Convoys to Russia

During this period the Royal Navy had been giving valuable assistance to our new ally Russia by sending supplies in convoy to the Russian port of Murmansk. This necessitated sailing ships along the German-occupied coast of Norway and within the Arctic Circle – shown on a polar chart as a circular parallel of latitude – the world's worst journey, as it has been described.

Some of the most exciting actions of the war took place on these journeys, when German aircraft and U-boats were a constant threat, whilst always in the background was the possibility of an attack on our convoys by the battle cruiser *Scharnhorst* and other heavy ships.[1] After their escape through the English Channel it was known that they were in Norwegian waters, where they strengthened the German fleet already there. In June 1942 one of our convoys (PQ. 17) was ordered to scatter when it was thought that an attack was about to be made by the *Tirpitz*.

[1] The *Gneisenau* had been severely damaged by a mine during her escape from Brest, and also by RAF bombers, and never went to sea again.

The attack did not occur, but our scattered merchant ships were badly mauled by both German aircraft and U-boats, 23 out of the convoy of 34 ships being sunk.

On another occasion, on 31st December 1942, Captain Sherbrooke, commanding the destroyer HMS *Onslow* and serving as Senior Officer to a destroyer squadron escorting an important convoy, made contact with an enemy squadron of vastly superior strength. Besides a destroyer force, the enemy had in company a pocket battleship and a cruiser. Our own destroyers had only 4.7-inch guns against the pocket battleship's 11-inch and the cruiser's 8-inch, but without hesitation Captain Sherbrooke led his destroyers into the attack against these overwhelming odds. Four times the enemy tried to force a gap in the convoy, and each time Captain Sherbrooke, with his destroyers, made the enemy retire behind a smokescreen.

Again the enemy attacked and again they were headed off by our destroyer force. The bridge of the *Onslow* was hit, a shell splinter striking Captain Sherbrooke in the eye, of which he lost the sight. Blood streamed from other wounds, but he would not receive medical attention and insisted on directing operations. Only when further hits on the *Onslow* forced Captain Sherbrooke to break off the action did he go below, where, as with Nelson at Trafalgar, the reports of the battle were brought to him. He was one of the 23 gallant men of the Navy in the Second World War who were awarded the Victoria Cross.

After some time heavier British ships came on the scene, but the Germans had had enough. They had received such a pummelling from our destroyers that the thought of British capital ships arriving was sufficient to send them back to their base.

The Sinking of the *Scharnhorst*

Exactly one year later the *Scharnhorst* sneaked out of harbour to attack one of our Russian convoys, but she was spotted by British cruisers and immediately turned for home. This time she was caught in a net, for units of the Home Fleet, including the battleship HMS *Duke of York*, had moved in to intercept her. Although the action which followed (31st December 1943) was fought in the darkness of the Arctic winter, accurate radar, effective gunnery and team work enabled the *Duke of York* to score hits at extreme range. In the end the *Scharnhorst* was sunk by torpedoes from the cruiser HMS *Jamaica*, sixty miles off the North Cape.

The End of the *Tirpitz*

It was known that Germany's new battleship, the *Tirpitz*, was moored in one of the Norwegian fjords, and as long as she remained afloat she was a potential menace to our Russian convoys. Plans were made to sink the warship, but because of her position, protected by submarine nets, the normal submarine was too big to carry out an attack. A development of the 'human torpedo' had produced a type of submarine known as the 'chariot'. It was manned by a crew of two, who sat astride the submarine, rather as though riding a tandem, and who wore special diving suits. The chariot could creep slowly and silently underneath its target and, when in position, the crew would detach the explosive head and fix it magnetically to the ship's bottom. The plan devised to sink the *Tirpitz* was that two of these chariots should be secured under the hull of a fishing vessel and taken to within easy reach of the battleship. British crews were to man the chariots, while the task of taking them to the *Tirpitz* was entrusted to a Norwegian skipper, Andreas Larsen. Already he had made over 50 trips from England to Norway, taking ammunition, arms and stores to help his fellow-countrymen in their underground resistance movement against the enemy. The British crews were hidden under a cargo of peat, and with forged ship's papers the fishing vessel made her way to Alten Fjord, the home of the *Tirpitz*. A German patrol vessel stopped the boat and inspected her, but the British charioteers lay hidden behind a false bulkhead, and she was allowed to pass on her way. The weather became foul and when the time came for the chariots to be released it was found that they had been swept away by the heavy seas. The vessel was immediately scuttled and all the crew got safely across the Swedish frontier except Able Seaman Evans, who was wounded in a brush with a German patrol. Later, on the express orders of Hitler, Evans was shot. Skipper Larsen and the rest of the crew managed to get back to England. The exploits of this Norwegian alone would fill a book and, but for the fact that only a British subject is allowed the highest honour, Skipper Larsen would have received the VC. But, apart from the decorations awarded by other countries, he received the Conspicuous Gallantry Medal, the DSO, the DSC and the DSM and bar. He is said to possess more decorations for wartime achievements than any other person in the Royal Navy. Naturally, he became one of Norway's national heroes.

In September 1943 X-craft, or midget submarines, were towed by bigger submarines to the area and were then released in an attack on the *Tirpitz*. They hacked their way through the submarine netting and – though some of them had great difficulty in wriggling through other obstructions surrounding the *Tirpitz* – two X-craft succeeded in attaching two fused charges to the hull of the battleship. The crews of the X-craft then scuttled their submarines and swam for the shore. An explosion followed which put out of action the main engine of the *Tirpitz*. The six survivors from all the X-craft involved were made prisoners by the Germans and all were decorated, two of them being awarded the VC. Ultimately the *Tirpitz* was sunk, while still in harbour, by heavy bombers of the RAF.

THE ALLIES ADVANCE

In the very month in which the X-craft were preparing for their attack on the *Tirpitz*, British and Canadian troops were landing on the beaches of Salerno, in Italy. In the previous month our armies had forced the enemy out of North Africa, and by July Sicily had been invaded by Allied forces. Nearly 3000 ships and vessels took part, from the largest battleship to the smallest landing craft, whilst overhead 4000 aircraft covered the landings. In August American troops entered Messina and the Sicilian campaign was over. But Salerno was a harder nut to crack. The day before the landings Italy had surrendered; thereafter opposition in that country came entirely from the Germans, and so was much tougher. The guns of the battleships *Warspite* and *Valiant*, however, restored the situation and Allied armies entered Naples in October. In Malta five Italian battleships, nine cruisers and fourteen destroyers surrendered to the British Commander-in-Chief, Admiral Cunningham, who signalled, 'The Italian Fleet is now anchored under the guns of the fortress of Malta'. The Allied armies in Italy now began their task of driving the enemy northwards. Inside Russia, German armies had been halted in heroic fighting by the Russians; and in the Pacific, slowly but surely, the United States Fleet was establishing its superiority over the Japanese. With two victories – one in the Coral Sea and the other at Midway Island – the American fleet turned the tide against the Japanese. The 'Hinge of Fate' as Mr Churchill called it, was now oiled and turning in our favour, but as far as the Royal Navy was concerned the main landings – those in France – were yet to come.

Operation 'Overlord'

Germany expected, of course, an invasion of the French coast and had concentrated over 70 submarines in the Bay of Biscay in readiness to meet it. Every U-boat that showed itself was immediately attacked by our aircraft and those that tried to submerge were hunted mercilessly by A/S vessels. Under General Eisenhower, the Supreme Commander, Operation 'Overlord' had been planned for 5th June 1944, but bad weather caused the postponement of the landings on the beaches of Normandy. Twenty-four hours later, with only a slight improvement in the elements, the decision was made – the Allied landings would take place. With a terrific air and sea bombardment, Operation 'Overlord' was launched. Minesweepers cleared a way for the landing craft, which in great waves bore down on the beaches. Meanwhile from the sea six battleships, 23 cruisers and 104 destroyers blazed away at the enemy; and from above planes carried paratroops to be dropped behind the enemy lines. The landings were successful, but our armies had to have supplies and to make this task easier huge prefabricated harbours known as 'Mulberries' were towed to the landing beaches so that stores of all types could be disembarked at speed. Until Germany surrendered in May 1945, over 2000 merchant ships, escorted by the Royal Navy, made use of these artificial harbours. Victory in Europe (VE) Day was celebrated with intense relief by the British public, which had stood up so valiantly and for so long to the constant German air raids, flying bombs, and terrifying V2 rockets.

The Collapse of Japan

With the unconditional surrender of Germany, the Royal Navy could afford to give assistance to the Americans, who had borne the brunt of the war in the Pacific against the Japanese. Our armies in Burma forced the Japanese from the territory they had conquered, and methodically the American fleet seized key islands commanding the approaches to Japan itself.

Lying in the Johore Strait near the island of Singapore, in crystal-clear water, was the 10 000-ton Japanese battleship *Takao*. XE3, a midget submarine with a crew of four, was selected for an attack on this ship. Commanded by Lieutenant Ian Fraser, the X-craft slithered through a gap in the anti-submarine net and wormed its way right underneath the keel of the *Takao*. Lieutenant Fraser had to work fast, for with an ebbing tide his vessel might be crushed by the huge battleship if operations lasted too long. Leading Seaman 'Mick' Magennis was already in his frogman's suit. He waited in the flooding chamber and then found there was so little space to spare below the warship's keel that he could not get the exit hatch wide open. He did, however, squeeze through the gap and commenced to attach limpet mines to the warship. But barnacles on the hull of the *Takao* made this difficult and so the slow process of chipping the ship's bottom had to be undertaken. The charges were attached along the bottom of the ship in six places and, exhausted and with his hands bleeding, Magennis made his way back to the X-craft, where he collapsed. Now came the job of getting out, but no matter how Lieutenant Fraser tried, wriggling this way and that, the X-craft would not budge. Suddenly, without warning, the midget submarine shot astern and broke surface. Only then was it realised that the box which had contained the limpet mines was still secured to the hull of the submarine, whereas it should have detached itself automatically. With the box still there, control of the X-craft was impossible. Leading Seaman Magennis exhausted as he was, volunteered to remove the obstacle, and within ten minutes the box was freed and he was back in the X-craft. Now for the escape, with the mines ticking away dangerously close, and at nine in the evening – fifty-two hours after starting out on their mission – the X-craft got away, undetected. Just about that time the mines exploded, tearing the bottom out of the warship. Lieutenant Fraser and Leading Seaman Magennis were each awarded the VC for their gallant conduct. The other two members of the crew received the DSO and the CGM respectively.

Within a few weeks of the surrender of Germany, a British Pacific Fleet was formed against Japan, but suddenly, with the dropping of atomic bombs on Japan itself, the Japanese surrendered. By August 1945 the Second World War was over. Over six years of hard fighting and bitter suffering the Allies had won a great victory over enslavement, and the whole world rejoiced.

THE UNITED NATIONS

The framework of the United Nations was in being even before the end of the war, and a few months after the Japanese surrender this organisation formally came into existence. There were fifty founder members (a number which had been increased to sixty by 1955), all of whom professed to have the primary object of promoting friendship among nations in the hope that future wars might be prevented. The responsibility for the maintenance of peace and security was given to the Security Council of the United Nations, a body of eleven members, five of which (China, France, the United Kingdom, USA and the USSR) were to be permanent members.

The inclusion of the USSR as a member of the Security Council showed how greatly Russia had grown in power during the war. From the time of the Russian Revolution in 1917 the doctrine of Communism had been adopted by the new republic; and slowly but methodically through the years this doctrine had spread far and wide, even in democratic countries. During the course of the Second World War many European countries were forcibly incorporated in the Soviet Union. Farther afield, particularly in China, the new doctrine of Communism had taken root in fertile soil. Even before the Second World War, Mao Tse Tung, the leader of the Chinese Communists, had declared his intention of ridding China of General Chiang Kai Shek and his Chinese Nationalist supporters. Once Japan was defeated, Mao Tse Tung built up a stronghold in North China and, with the assistance of Russian arms, surrounded himself with a powerful army. Very soon this new Communist force had taken Manchuria, Peking and Tientsin. By January 1949 Chiang Kai Shek had resigned office as President, and the Nationalist Government rapidly declined as province after province was occupied by Communist forces.

THE 'AMETHYST' EPISODE

By January, 1949, Chinese Communist forces were separated from the Nationalists by the Yangste River and 200 miles up this river from

Shanghai was the Nationalist capital of Nanking. All foreign embassies to China had their offices in Nanking and as routine, the Royal Navy kept a frigate on a regular duty tour in Nanking to keep contact with our own Embassy Staff. In the January the warship which had this duty was HMS *Consort* and she was due to be relieved by HMS *Amethyst* which was already moving along the river for the change-over.

En route, she was fired upon by guns of the Chinese Communist shore batteries and the Commanding Officer of HMS *Amethyst*, a Lt. Commander Skinner was mortally wounded by the attack. HMS *Consort*, having been warned of the attack, made full speed from Nanking to assist her, but she too was subjected to murderous gunfire from Communist gun-batteries. Meanwhile, HMS *London*, a cruiser carrying 8-inch guns, and the frigate, HMS *Black Swan*, were approaching Shanghai in order to pay a pre-arranged courtesy visit. They too received news of the unprovoked attack on the other British warships and they immediately steamed to assist, only to receive similar treatment from the Communist shore batteries. Because the range from the river to the shore was so short, it proved extremely difficult for the heavy-calibre 8-inch guns of HMS *London* to be depressed to such a low elevation and, moreover, the ship herself was hit repeatedly. With many casualties aboard and considerable damage to her structure, she was obliged to return to Shanghai for repairs.

HMS *Amethyst*, meanwhile, with casualties of her own, had taken temporary refuge in an anchorage on the river where she could attend to her wounded and carry out emergency repairs to the ship. Whilst at anchor, a Royal Air Force Sunderland Flying boat, with a Royal Air Force Doctor and medical supplies, managed to land alongside HMS *Amethyst* and get aid to the wounded. In doing so however, the Sunderland was greeted with a hail of machine-gun bullets from Communist gun positions and the Sunderland was obliged to 'take-off'.

Eventually, a Lt Commander Kerans, who was the Assistant Naval Attache at Nanking, with the friendly assistance of Chinese National Forces, managed to make his way overland to the shore nearest to the ship and by devious ways boarded the vessel and took over her command. There followed months of almost daily talks with the local Commanders of the Chinese Communist forces with the hope that they would grant the ship a safe passage to Shanghai – but all proved in vain.

In consequence, Commander Kerans told his ship's Company that he planned to run the gauntlet of the Chinese shore batteries and make a dash for it. One night, the *Amethyst* slipped her moorings and commenced her hazardous trip to safety – 150 miles away. The story of this remarkable escape has been the source of many books and even a film. Suffice it to relate here that despite all the hair-raising events which occurred, the *Amethyst* did escape.

'Us be pround of ee' was how the event was greeted by a group of

Plymouth Wrens. The news of the escape electrified the world's press and when the crews of all the ships involved in this Yangste incident returned to the United Kingdom, they marched through the streets of London amidst cheering crowds to an official banquet in their honour at the Guildhall.

THE KOREAN WAR

The first real test to the newly-formed United Nations came as a result of the invasion of South Korea by North Korean Forces in June 1950. Attempts had been made previously to unify North and South Korea, but due to Russian intransigence this failed and when the attack occurred, the Security Council of the United Nations met and discussed the issue and finally ordered the North Koreans to withdraw their troops.

Russia did not agree with this order and so the Council called on all other members for their support. American occupation forces in Japan were quickly despatched to assist the South Koreans and the British Government promised military assistance. Before this could be effected, however, the South Korean capital of Seoul had been captured by the invaders. Eventually, British, Australian, Canadian and New Zealand naval forces joined with the US Navy in patrolling the Korean coastline to prevent supplies reaching North Korea by sea. Military operations were put under the command of an American soldier, General McArthur and he mounted an offensive against North Korea. In this he was assisted by Commonwealth troops and Royal Marine Commandos who had been flown out from Plymouth in the August of 1950.

The following October, the Chinese Government declared that they would not stand idle if North Korea were invaded and they stationed on the borders of North Korea and China large concentrations of their own forces. Meanwhile, diplomatic efforts were taking place to effect a peaceful solution and in July, 1951, truce talks began.

It was not however until 1953 that peace was achieved. During the war, over 75 warships of the Royal and Commonwealth Navies had been engaged in fighting for varied periods and apart from the devastation and suffering caused by this unprovoked conflict, there were more than 3 000 000 casualties on both sides.

When peace came, there was no real friendly outcome because the political division between North and South Korea remained as before. Nevertheless, the war did show that the force of Communist China was one to be reckoned with and no more would China be content to remain unconcerned with events on her borders. On the other hand, the war demonstrated close liaison of the UN Forces and how effectively they had worked in harmony.

THE SUEZ CRISIS OF 1956

Really to appreciate the reasons behind the Anglo-French landings at Port Said in 1956, some of the past history of this troubled zone should be understood. The 100-mile Suez Canal, linking the Mediterranean with the shorter route to India and the Far East, had been guarded by Great Britain under a Treaty arrangement with Egypt since 1869. In carrying out this obligation, British troops occupied garrison towns in various centres along the length and breadth of the important waterway, ensuring that ships of all nations could make their peaceful progress. These centres were almost miniature British towns, housing the families of British soldiers. To show that it was not intended that British protection was to be permanent, a treaty was signed with Egypt in 1936 allowing the protection to continue for 20 years from that date, by which time it was expected that Egyptian forces would be capable of relieving the British soldiers.

In June, 1952, the situation changed dramatically as Egyptian troops overthrew King Farouk's control of Egypt and declared the country a Republic. As this move might have threatened the control of the canal, Britain reinforced the whole zone with more troops. British families living in the zone were advised to return home though there was no compulsion, and as might be expected there was great speculation as to what might happen. Diplomatic activity between Egypt and Great Britain increased and there were many comments on the situation from countries not directly concerned, in particular from the Soviet Union who were openly sympathetic to any view expressed by the Egyptians. The outcome of such diplomatic negotiations was that Great Britain reaffirmed the agreement made in the 1936 Treaty with Egypt, namely that she would hand over the guardianship of the canal to Egypt in 1956.

On the agreed date British troops commenced their withdrawal and a Colonel Gamal Abdul Nasser, the leader of the new Egyptian Republic, assumed office as President and took the salute at a 'Victory' parade in Cairo to celebrate the British withdrawal. One of his first steps was to 'nationalise' the canal and, flushed with this success, he set about furthering the cause of Arab unity by despatching his army to invade the neighbouring State of Israel. Formerly called Palestine, it had been a troubled area for many years, but the League of Nations after the First World War decided that it was a most suitable home for people of the Jewish faith. Originally Arab territory, the Egyptians were suspicious of the intentions of Israel, hence Colonel Nasser's intention to champion the cause of Arab unity.

Britain and France demanded that both Egypt and Israel should stop all warlike actions but by that time Israeli forces had actually advanced over 50 miles inside Egyptian territory. Fearing that the safety of the canal was at serious risk Anglo-French military intervention occurred on

November 5th. Paratroopers were dropped near key Egyptian positions and on the following day the British carriers HMS *Bulwark* and HMS *Albion* together with supporting warships of the Mediterranean Squadron arrived off Port Said at the northern end of the canal. Royal Marine Commandos were landed in assault craft and 'Whirlwind' helicopters from the carriers HMS *Ocean* and HMS *Theseus* transported other Commandos ashore. By the end of the day, Port Said had been captured and Allied forces had advanced southwards along the canal.

The United Nations Council was quick to react at the action and demanded the immediate withdrawal of Anglo-French forces and their replacement by an international United Nations force with orders to maintain peace. And so the Suez affair came to an end just over seven days after it had started. Long enough however for the Egyptians to deny the use of the canal to any nation by sinking, in strategic places, blockships – vessels filled with concrete and scrap iron.

Later, under United Nations sponsorship, British, French and German salvage ships undertook to clear a channel through the waterway and reopen it to shipping but this was not achieved until the April of the following year.

As far as the Royal Navy was concerned, the Suez affair demonstrated the importance of an amphibious operation and the versatile role of the helicopter – facts which led to the conversion of the carriers *Bulwark* and *Albion* to carry Royal Marine Commandos and their amphibious craft and squadrons of naval helicopters.

PART TWO

CHAPTER NINE

The Royal Marines

No history of the Navy, however condensed, could be written without particular mention of the Royal Marines.

From earliest days it had been common practice to include soldiers as part of a ship's complement. In Drake's voyage round the world in 1577–80 the soldier, or Elizabethan 'gentleman adventurer', came in for special reference: in a famous speech Sir Francis said, 'I must have the gentleman to hale and draw with the mariner, and the mariner with the gentleman'. In simple English Drake was stating a very real truth, namely, that if sailors and soldiers were to serve in the same ship, both must remember that they were all of the one company – a maxim which is equally true today.

In 1660, when the monarchy was restored in the person of Charles II, the proportion of soldiers to seamen had dropped steadily. An attempt to restore this balance was made by the king's brother, James, Duke of York, who held the post of Lord High Admiral when war with Holland broke out again. This new regiment of sea-soldiers was thus known as 'the Duke of York and Albany's Maritime Regiment of Foot' or 'the Admiral's regiment'; but sailors, so alive to nicknames, christened them 'the yellow regiment' because of the colour of their uniforms. Many of the men for the new regiment were raised from the trained bands of the city of London and on account of their Cockney cheerfulness they received yet another nickname, the 'Jollies', a name which has survived to the present day. They served with great distinction at the famous sea-battle of Scheveningen in 1653. Thirty-two years later James himself became king of England as James II; during his three-year reign the colour of the uniforms of his marine regiments was changed from yellow to red.

After three protracted wars against the Dutch, peace was signed with Holland. The throne of England was then offered to Prince William of Orange, who had married Mary, the daughter of James. The king himself took refuge in France, where Louis XIV provided money and men in an attempt to restore him to the throne. The War of the League of Augsburg followed, the first conflict in a series of struggles with France that was to last for a hundred years.[1]

---

[1] See page 17.

THE MARINES IN THE CENTURY OF WARS WITH FRANCE

In this lengthy period, soldiers or marines from various regiments served afloat with the Royal Navy. In the War of the League of Augsburg the Earls of Torrington and Pembroke raised soldiers for sea service, and these served with Admiral Russell at the battle of Barfleur, when a French fleet was defeated. It was in this war, in 1694, that the marines were first mentioned as being exercised at the 'great guns'.

In this century of wars with France – which at sea ranged from home waters to the West Indies, Canada and America, and from European shores to Australia – marines and sea-soldiers were always in evidence.[1] At a later date they were absorbed into various Army infantry units – the East Lancs., the East Surreys, the Duke of Cornwall's Light Infantry, the Royal Warwickshire Fusiliers, the Green Howards, the Lancashire Fusiliers, the Border Regiment, to mention a few – but they never forget their earlier association with the Royal Navy as sea-soldiers. Some of the modern counterparts of these regiments still keep alive this connection with their past history. One in particular, the East Surrey Regiment, drinks and health of Her Majesty sitting down – a custom which dates back to the time when deck-heads were very low.[2] As all regiments concerned were 'foot' soldiers, they continued to wear red uniforms at times, much to the amusement of their sailor comrades who, possessing no official uniform of their own, would quite frequently refer to the marines as 'red-faced lobsters'.

Gibraltar, 1704

Striking evidence of their duties in landing parties is seen in the capture of Gibraltar in 1704, during the War of the Spanish Succession – yet another conflict in the century-long struggle with France. On the death of the king of Spain in 1700 France virtually annexed the Spanish kingdom, together with all Spain's possessions across the seas. This enlarged the task of the Royal Navy, for the war with France now meant a conflict with Spain too. A new British naval base nearer to the coast of Spain was essential. Portsmouth, Devonport and Chatham were all very well as naval bases in a war against France alone; but now the enemy coastline had been extended considerably, and it was

[1] There is a distinction between regiments raised as marines and those raised for sea-service. (They were then known by the names of their Colonels – the numbers came later.) In 1702 six regiments were ordered to be raised as marines and six more for sea-service. The marine regiments were the 30th, 31st and 32nd; the other three were disbanded in 1713. The 4th (then known as Seymour's, also as The Queen's Own – which was *not* the later 2nd Foot) was also a marine regiment, but was returned to the line in 1711. The sea-service regiments were the 6th, 19th, 20th, 34th, 35th and 36th.

[2] In 1964 the Sovereign directed that, to mark their tercentenary, the Royal Marines should in future drink the Loyal Toast seated in all R.M. messes, ashore and afloat.

unreasonable to expect British men-of-war damaged in attacks upon Spanish ports and ships to return to home waters for repairs. The Spanish port of Cadiz was selected as the most suitable base, but the attempt to take it was fruitless. Admiral Rooke, who commanded the expedition, decided as a last resort to attack Gibraltar, a barren rock held by some 80 Spanish soldiers. It was certainly not a great number, but anyone who has seen the famous rock will realise that its very composition and situation render it suitable for defence with small forces. The Spaniards thought it impregnable – but they had not reckoned with the marines!

Before daylight on the 23rd July 1704 the British fleet, having taken up its station, received a signal from Admiral Rooke to bombard the rock. Fifteen thousand shot were fired in five or six hours into the enemy gun positions guarding the mole head, forcing the Spaniards to retreat to gun emplacements higher up the rock. Pressing home this temporary advantage, orders were given to Captain Whitaker and a landing party of seamen to seize the town. The enemy had prepared for this eventuality, and from their secure positions high above they fought tenaciously against the landing party, which, however, after many setbacks was successful in overpowering the Spaniards. Another landing party, this time of marines, received the formal surrender of the fortress. The story, however, did not end there, for during the following eight months French and Spanish troops tried again and again to recapture Gibraltar. Two thousand marines had been left ashore as a defending garrison and, despite the attempts of the enemy – sometimes with as many as fifteen thousand troops – the marines remained resolute in the defence of the 'gateway to the Mediterranean'.

This superb feat of endurance under very trying conditions has been judged by historians as the highlight of our sea-soldiers' history – in fact, the only battle honour worn on the colours of the Corps is simply 'Gibraltar'.

The New Corps of Marines

After this war a short 'breathing spell' followed, during which both sides began to prepare for the next round. Gibraltar had been taken, as well as the island of Minorca in the Mediterranean, but no major defeat of France and Spain had been achieved. During these many periods of inactivity in the long struggle with France, both seamen and marines were paid off, for the country found it uneconomic to employ soldiers and sailors during temporary lulls in fighting. However, it was obvious to the leading Admirals of the day that there was a pressing requirement for a regular body of marines under Admiralty control and specifically trained for sea service. On 5th April 1755 an Order in Council provided for the creation of fifty companies of Marines. This new Corps was divided into three groups, based at the naval ports of Chatham, Portsmouth and Plymouth respectively. The new Corps took part in every naval engagement which followed. Marines were with General Wolfe at Quebec and Admiral Hawke at Quiberon Bay – in the first instance as a landing party and in the second as musketeers stationed on the upper deck.

The century of wars with France culminated in the American War of Independence, during which two battalions of Marines were sent to Boston. It is interesting to note that, although the colonists won their independence from Great Britain in this war, one of the first steps of their newly-appointed Congress in 1775 was to create a Marine Corps of their own, the forerunner of the present United States Marine Corps.

THE MARINES IN THE WAR AGAINST REVOLUTIONARY FRANCE

The year 1789 completed the hundred-year struggle with France, yet that very year heralded another war, this time against the French Revolution. The naval actions which ensued have already been described, but it must be remembered that in each of these the Marines played their part. Their quarters on board were kept apart from the seamen's messdeck, and in periods of peace they were given a variety of responsible duties such as acting as sentries outside the Captain's cabin and the spirit or rum store and – perhaps the most important of all – the protection of the ships' magazine.

After the battle of Cape St. Vincent in 1797, and in particular during the naval mutinies of the same year, Admiral Sir John Jervis (later, Earl St. Vincent) was so impressed with the Marines' loyal behaviour that he wrote, 'There never was any appeal made to them for honour, courage or loyalty that they did not more than realise my expectations. If ever the hour of real danger should come to England, the Marines will be found the country's sheet anchor'. Their integrity as a Corps was an established fact, and many naval captains put this to good effect by messing marines between the officers and the sailors. This was a precautionary measure to prevent mutiny, and such was their acknowledged fidelity that this custom became universal in men-of-war during Nelson's time.

The 'Royal Marines'

On 29th April 1802 King George III, at the request of Lord St. Vincent, was pleased to grant the Corps the title of 'Royal Marines', and in honour of this royal regard the facings of their uniforms were changed to blue.

During the Napoleonic War the strength of the Corps was at times as high as 20 000; and in a typical 'first-rate', i.e. of 100 guns, one would have found in charge of the Royal Marines contingent, a Royal Marines captain assisted usually by two lieutenants of the Corps. Together they were responsible for some 120 non-commissioned officers and men. In action the marines worked with the guns' crews. In periods of peace they acted as sentries, ships' policemen and often as personal servants to officers. In 1815, ten years after Trafalgar, the Duke of Wellington and the Prussian Marshal Blücher defeated the French armies at Waterloo, and Napoleon was banished to the island of St. Helena, HMS *Bellerophon* conveyed him into exile, and when the famous Frenchman inspected the detachment of Royal Marines on board he remarked, 'One might do much with 100 000 soldiers such as these'.

The Royal Marine Artillery

Nelson himself had always pressed the Admiralty for marines to be trained as artillerymen, and the year 1804 saw the formation of the Royal Marine Artillery (RMA) as a regular feature of the Corps. To each of the three port divisions an artillery company was added, and from this new activity emerged a home for the RMA at Woolwich and later at Eastney Barracks, Portsmouth. When Nelson was mortally wounded at Trafalgar, he was carried below by Sergeant Secker, RM.

FROM WATERLOO TO THE FIRST WORLD WAR

In 1827 George IV granted the badge of the globe and laurel to the Royal Marines as the 'most proper and distinctive badge', for no colours or crest could possibly contain the names of all the battles in which the Corps had taken part, both at sea and on land.

One of the three VCs awarded to Royal Marines during the Crimean War of 1854 was awarded to Lt. Dowell, RMA, who showed great bravery when under heavy fire from Russian batteries in the Baltic. When the British fleet was bombarding the port of Viborg, Lt. Dowell was instrumental in saving the crew of a naval cutter which was transferring ammunition from one of our warships.

The Royal Marine Light Infantry

Another distinction was gained by the Corps in 1855 – that the Royal Marines would in future be a 'light' corps. This was a much-prized title and only one other regiment of the time[1] shared this honour – the 32nd Regiment, which was made Light Infantry in 1859 for its defence of the

[1] There were, however, several other regiments of the line before this date which also bore the title 'Light Infantry'.

Residency at Lucknow during the Indian Mutiny. As light infantry, the bugle or light infantry 'horn' was adopted as a badge for all ranks. The uniform was somewhat similar to that of the Foot Guards except that a dark blue or white helmet was worn instead of a bearskin. In true Marine tradition they were trained both for service afloat and with the Army as a brigade. The Royal Marine Light Infantry and the Royal Marine Artillery together made up the Royal Marine Forces until they were amalgamated in 1923.

The Royal Marines Band Service

Bands had existed in the Royal Navy from very early days, though they were composed mainly of foreigners; but not until 1846 did the Admiralty officially recognise the naval rating of 'bandsman'. So many marines were attracted to naval bands that at the turn of the century, in 1903, the provision of bands for service both in ships and on shore was entrusted to the Royal Marines, who took this duty very seriously and formed their School of Music at Eastney. It remained there until 1930, when it was transferred to its present home at Deal.

THE FIRST WORLD WAR

At the outbreak of hostilities against Germany in 1914 Royal Marines served both as members of the RMA and the RMLI. Their versatility in both roles is shown in the places where they fought. The first RMA anti-aircraft batteries, as well as heavy 15-inch howitzers, went into action in France in April 1915; wherever Army regiments fought so did detachments of the RMA – even in German West Africa. At sea, members of the RMLI played their part with the Royal Navy at Coronel, the Falkland Isles, the Battle of the Dogger Bank and at Jutland, as well as in defensively armed merchant ships.

Jutland

At Jutland, on 31st May 1916, some 5800 Royal Marines served in the Grand Fleet, nearly 600 of whom were to lose their lives in this large-scale action. Serving on board Beatty's flagship, HMS *Lion*, was Major Harvey, of the RMLI. In the chase by the *Lion* of the German battle cruisers, Major Harvey's gun turret position was hit and he was mortally wounded. With great presence of mind, though his life was fast ebbing, he gave the order for the flooding of the magazine, thereby saving his ship and his comrades. For his great devotion to duty he received the posthumous award of the Victoria Cross.

The Zeebrugge Raid

On St. George's Day (23rd April) 1918, Admiral Sir Roger Keyes made his daring raid on Zeebrugge, a port in Belgium whence U-boats made their entrance into the North Sea. Covered by the guns of accompanying warships, the Royal Marines stormed the mole, while others blocked and destroyed the harbour. Captain E. Bamford, DSO, was one of the landing party from HMS *Vindictive.* While ashore on the mole and under heavy fire, he displayed the greatest initiative in command of his company and in his complete disregard for danger by leading an attack on an enemy battery. For his act of most conspicuous gallantry he was awarded the Victoria Cross.

While this action was proceeding, Sergeant N A Finch, RMA was second-in-command of a pom-pom and Lewis gun station in the foretop of the *Vindictive*, which was giving protective cover to the landings. At one time the ship was being hit every few seconds by enemy shore batteries, but Sergeant Finch's gun position kept up a continuous return fire, rapidly changing from one enemy target to another. Unfortunately, two heavy shells made a direct hit on this foretop post and Sergeant Finch found himself the only surviving member of the gun's crew in this battered and exposed spot; but, undaunted, he got a Lewis gun into action and kept firing until another direct hit silenced his position. Miraculously, he survived this episode and lived to receive the Victoria Cross.

Such is the modesty of the Corps that in the battalion diary covering the raid on Zeebrugge only the following appears: '23rd April, St. George's Day: operation carried out; *Vindictive* reached mole 8.15 a.m. Battalion arrived Dover 10.30 a.m.' But casualties speak for themselves, for out of the 700 Marines embarked for the raid, 119 were killed, 234 wounded and 12 taken prisoner – in other words, one man out of every two either lost his life or became a casualty or prisoner. It was the 4th Battalion RM that had the honour of storming Zeebrugge, and as a fitting tribute to their valour it was then decided that no future Royal Marine battalion would ever be called the '4th Battalion'.

King George V, paying tribute to the record of the Corps in 1918, declared, 'Everywhere your Corps has added fresh glory to its record, and never has your name stood higher than today. I am prouder than ever to be your Colonel-in-Chief'. Besides their varied activities during the First World War, the Corps also supplied pilots to the Royal Naval Air Service and to the Royal Air Force when it was first instituted, in April 1918. In November of the same year, when the armistice was declared, 57 000 officers and men belonged to the Royal Marine Forces – a number which was reduced to about 19 000 after demobilisation.

The Royal Marines between the two World Wars

In common with the other Services, drastic economies were enforced on the Royal Marines after the war, and in 1923, it was decided to amalgamate the two branches, the RMA and the RMLI, under the old title 'The Royal Marines'. The Gosport headquarters of the RMLI was taken over by the Admiralty for boys' training as HMS *St. Vincent* – but since boys are now no longer enlisted for naval service, HMS *St. Vincent* has closed. Some of the buildings remain together with new ones as the site is now a State Comprehensive School, *St. Vincent* by name! The RMLI had been nicknamed the 'Red Marines' because of the scarlet hue in their tunics, while the RMA, with their artillery blue, were called the 'Blue Marines'. But with their newly-acquired singleness the former friendly rivalry between the 'Reds' and the 'Blues' disappeared, never to return.

THE SECOND WORLD WAR

At the outbreak of the Second World War the total strength of the Royal Marines was only 12 000. Economies between the wars had produced this result, and when the new world war occurred the Royal Marines found it difficult at first to fulfil all their obligations. Their primary task was the manning of the Fleet, and in performing this duty they served in every type of vessel with the exception of submarines. At the early naval action, the Battle of the River Plate, Lieut. De'ath, RM was awarded the DSO for his gallantry in dealing with fires when a gun turret in HMS *Ajax* was hit by shellfire from the German pocket battleship *Admiral Graf Spee*. In the same action Marine Russel, on board HMS *Exeter*, with his left forearm blown away and his right arm shattered, remained at his post encouraging his comrades. The Royal Marines were in the thick of the action alongside their sailor comrades, and this is true for every sea action which follows – the Norwegian Campaign, the Battle of Narvik, Dunkirk, the sinking of the *Bismarck*, the Mediterranean campaign and the final 'D' Day landings.

Raising of Shore Formations

Ashore, new moves were afoot to increase the versatility of the Corps. It had been approved that the Royal Marine Brigade should be increased to divisional strength, and for this purpose new battalions were raised. One of these new formations was given the initials MNBDO (Mobile Naval Base Defence Organisation), a long title for a very important job, the defence of naval bases overseas. These duties included the manning of anti-aircraft guns and searchlight positions and the provision of transport units and infantry battalions, the latter to take care of possible enemy parachutists. Another new name to appear was the Royal Marine Siege Regiment, which manned the heavy guns mounted on railway lines in the Dover area. The first of the new detachments with the many initials served with distinction in the Mediterranean, at the landings in Crete, and later as a rearguard when we were obliged to leave the island. In this action, out of the 2200 marines who were landed only 1,000 returned in the evacuation.

Combined Operations – 'Commandos'

Amphibious landing parties were the natural function of the Royal Marines, but so many calls had been made on their services, particularly with the Royal Navy, that not until April 1942 were they able to take up Commando work. The word 'Commando' first became familiar during the South African War, when guerilla tactics were used by the Boers with great success. The 'Commandos', or bands of fighting men, relied on small-scale, swift attacks without the burden of supply columns, and quite often their successes were due to surprise and the capture of the arms and equipment of the enemy. Many improvements in small arms had been made since the Boer War, but nevertheless the basic idea of a self-sufficient force, physically fit and able to forage for itself, appealed to General Dill, who was Chief of the Imperial General Staff in 1940.

To Winston Churchill, the Prime Minister in the dark days after Dunkirk, the introduction of Commandos into the British Army seemed a useful way of exercising the offensive spirit of our troops once again. Official sanction was thus given to this new enterprise, and in the first instance an officer, usually under the age of 40, was given the task of forming his Commando unit. He selected his men from volunteers, and then the whole unit, originally no more than 70 strong, would undergo rigorous training in which they were taught to use knives and small arms, to live off the land and generally fend for themselves. Once proficient, they were then introduced to their counterparts in the Royal Navy, the officers and ratings who commanded the raiding flotillas – small, fast motor boats and assault craft. Together they exercised in practice landings, and finally a rehearsal followed for a landing on an enemy shore – a dash to the landing beach, a few hectic minutes of fighting ashore, following by a return to base. Such was the training of our early Commandos – men at the peak of physical fitness, ready for anything and determined to strike a blow at the enemy. With their faces blackened, their uniforms camouflaged, and expert in the use of Sten guns and knives, they were to cause the enemy many a shock. They were essentially 'volunteer' units, and each man retained the right to return to his own regiment should he think Commando work too much for him – but few ever did.

The Dieppe Raid

In Chapter 8 a short account was given of the raid on St. Nazaire in March 1942. A further raid on the enemy-occupied port of Dieppe had been planned also by the Chief of Combined Operations, Lord Louis Mountbatten. Together with Army Commandos, 40 Commando RM took part in this daring exploit, on 19th August 1942. It was officially reported that the Royal Marines went in to land 'with a courage terrible to see, determined, if Fortune so wished, to repeat at Dieppe what their fathers had done at Zeebrugge'. But Fate decided otherwise: Dieppe proved to be too heavily defended and a rain of shells, mortar bombs and machine-gun fire met the first wave of Commandos as they came ashore. The Commander of the unit, Lieutenant-Colonel J P P Phillipps, who was one of the first to land, realising that the defences were too strong, stood on the shore in full view of the enemy and signalled other landing craft to turn back. Whilst doing so the Colonel, who was already wounded, received a spurt of machine-gun fire in the stomach and fell dying. His gallant action prevented the death roll, which was already very heavy, from becoming even bigger.

Royal Marine Commandos in Sicily and Italy

After many setbacks the tide turned in favour of the Allies in 1942, when the island of Madagascar was captured from the Vichy French – yet another event in which Royal Marines played a prominent part. At the close of the same year Allied landings in North Africa were already showing useful results, and by the spring of 1943, with the Germans and Italians in full retreat from North Africa, we were contemplating the invasion of both Sicily and Italy. On 10th July 1943, 40 Commando RM had the honour of being the first seaborne troops to land on the shores of Sicily. By August the Sicilian campaign was over, and in the following month the landings at Salerno took place, in which 41 Commando RM took part. The Italians surrendered almost simultaneously with the landings on their soil, but the RM Commandos found the resulting German opposition much tougher. However, help came from their comrades in the Royal Navy and from the heavy guns of the battleships *Warspite* and *Valiant*, which were lying off shore. In a very short time the German coastal fortifications were destroyed and the situation restored. Before long the German armies were forced to retreat northwards.

Walcheren, November 1944

The part played by the Royal Navy in the famous 'D' Day landings has been described in Chapter 8. In those landings, Royal Marine Commandos, with their armoured support groups in Centaur tanks, broke the crust of the enemy resistance in Normandy. Although the 'Mulberry' harbours were doing a magnificent job, it was essential that the port of

Antwerp be freed of the enemy so that Allied ships might use it to bring essential supplies. Antwerp itself was captured by our armies in September 1944, but the enemy still held the approaches to the port from the island of Walcheren, in the estuary of the River Schelde. The task of smashing the German resistance fell largely to RM Commandos, and the 4th Commando Brigade, comprising 41, 47 and 48 Commando units, was selected for this honour. Assisted by the RAF and by landing and support craft manned in the main by Royal Marines, the three units made their assault on the island on 1st November 1944, a day which was to prove one of the most memorable in the history of the Corps. The enemy-held dykes bristled with pillboxes and guns varying in calibre from 3-in. to 8.7-in., but the Royal Navy, with their assault craft, ran right to the edges of the beaches, drawing the enemy fire and covering the landings of the Commandos. Some of the pillboxes were put out of action at point-blank range, and in the severe hand-to-hand fighting which followed casualties were very heavy. But the attack was pressed home and the German troops were overwhelmed. By this success the threat to the port of Antwerp was removed and progress to eventual victory was accelerated.

Corporal Tom Hunter, VC

By April 1945 the German forces in Italy had been forced steadily northwards, but in the area around the beautiful Lake of Comacchio enemy activity was still vigorous. 43 Commando RM, which had been engaged in driving the enemy from the islands off the coast of Yugoslavia, returned to the mainland of Italy with orders to crush this resistance in the Lake Comacchio area. In the attack which followed, Corporal Tom Hunter was in charge of a Bren gun troop. As he cautiously advanced to within a quarter of a mile of his objective, he observed that some German troops were holding a group of houses. The rest of his troop, who were behind him, were in the open and without cover. With this in mind, Corporal Hunter seized his Bren gun and charged across the open ground towards the German positions. Enemy fire came from all directions – from the housetops, from the windows and at ground level from the gardens – but Tom Hunter, undaunted, continued his dash towards the Germans, firing from the hip with great accuracy until he had completely demoralised the enemy. Although a burst of enemy fire killed him in the end, his action, which showed a complete disregard for the enemy fire, enabled the rest of his troop to reach and overpower the enemy. Tom Hunter was posthumously awarded the VC – the only Royal Marine to receive this most prized honour in the Second World War.

Among many other deeds of daring performed by individuals and small parties of marines one of the most exciting was the exploit of Major Hasler and Corporal Laver. In October 1942 Major Hasler was given the command of a canoe force equipped with explosives, and the task of destroying enemy shipping at the French port of Bordeaux, some 70 miles up the River Gironde, which flows into the middle of the Bay of Biscay. The whole force, comprising the crews of 5 two-man canoes, was launched from HMS/M *Tuna*, off the mouth of the river. Three of the canoes, or 'cockleshells', were lost in the approaches to the estuary, but two, with Major Hasler and Corporal Laver in respective command, reached Bordeaux after a journey which lasted three days and nights. They paddled their canoes by night and took refuge under cover by day, and succeeded in fixing their limpet mines to the hulls of many ships in the harbour of Bordeaux. Having severely damaged six large enemy vessels in this way, they made their escape through the neutral country of Spain. Of many other 'small expeditions' in which Royal Marines took part with the object of obtaining intelligence of the enemy, each displayed a high degree of courage and initiative, and each in its way contributed to final victory.

Anyone who has watched a Royal Marine band at Olympia or the Royal Tournament cannot fail to be impressed by their music and bearing, for efficiency in parade work is second to none with any Royal Marine. But how many realise that during the Second World War one bandsman out of four lost his life by enemy action – the highest percentage of casualties in any Service during the six years' struggle for freedom? In their varied ways, whether as bandsmen, commandos, cockleshell heroes or sea-soldiers, the Royal Marines continued, in the immortal words of Kipling, 'a-doin all kinds of things' to make victory certain.

THE ROYAL MARINES SINCE 1945

The Royal Marines emerged from the Second World War with yet another string to their bow, namely their Commando units. In October 1945 the Army Commandos were disbanded and Commando training passed exclusively to the Corps as being most qualified for this role. Their training centre is in the West country and there each intending commando undergoes an exhaustive course, including route marches, cliff assaults, judo training, the use of small arms – in fact, everything that will ensure fitness and the ability to meet the unexpected and to deal with it in a competent manner. The 3rd Commando Brigade, a complete entity with its arms, transport and equipment, is always ready to move at short notice – for this reason it is often called the 'fire-brigade'. Since the Second World War, wherever there has been trouble or the possibility of unrest and danger to British lives and property, the Commando Brigade has been there. In this protective role it has seen service in Hong Kong, Korea, Malaya, Egypt and, more recently, in

Cyprus. Whether landed from assault craft or – as at Suez in 1956 – from helicopters, RM Commandos have shared with our other forces in the safeguarding of British interests.

Today a Commando unit is much larger than when it was first instituted by the Army in the dark days of 1940 and now comprises over 600 officers, non-commissioned officers and men. These figures were determined in 1942, when Royal Marines first took part in Commando operations, and the present organisation of the Brigade is based similarly on the wartime establishment.

Pervading the whole Corps – whether ashore as commandos or at sea as sea-soldiers or bandsmen – is a strong sense of discipline, a discipline not based on fear but on a spirit of pride and confidence in what is very much a 'family' Corps. Throughout their history is found this hereditary pattern as sons follow their fathers into the Royals. With such strong family ties it is not surprising to learn that the Royal Corps looks after its members both on active service and in retirement. Old and young meet in the branches of the Royal Marines Association and talk of days past and present. And for the civilian, too, who has a regard for the Corps there is the RMR, a volunteer Reserve Unit which takes part with verve and relish in the many exercises organised annually with regular units. They may be requested to carry out a mock attack on a naval base, either from the sea or by land, and, as happens with their regular counterparts, this is planned to the last detail. Only the noise of their paddles or the brush of the undergrowth will reveal their presence as, with blackened faces, they converge towards their objective. It is a life that offers adventure, excitement and travel, but, above all, the service of one's country.

The Corps today numbers about 8000 officers and men all trained commandos· ready to go into action anywhere, from the humid jungle to the frozen wastes of the Arctic. In the past they have served in all parts of the world. Today, with Britain's frontiers much nearer home, the green beret is more frequently seen on the flanks of NATO, from the Arctic Circle to Turkey, ready to quell any trouble and to help in time of disasters such as floods or earthquakes. As amphibious experts, Royal Marines man the Navy's landing craft from large tank landing craft to small glass-fibre raiders, and as ship-borne commandos, they serve in small detachments to land and restore order in trouble spots. Those who specialise in mountain and arctic warfare are trained to live and fight in temperatures of minus 40 degrees Centigrade. Situations and locations will alter in common with the changing history of nations; but no matter where the future Royal Marine may find himself, he can look forward to a very versatile career in a Service which has had a most notable and glorious history, but which, like the Royal Navy, is ever alive to accept new challenges.

CHAPTER TEN

The Language and Customs of the Navy

So many of our everyday expressions, which even in this nuclear age still make a sailor's conversation unique, have their origins in the past history of the Navy or in the doings of its great men that it is worth our while not only to understand their sources but also to preserve them.

As we might expect, many expressions peculiar to sailing ships have already disappeared, but many still remain and are used every day in the Service. There is only room here to list a small proportion of those in most common use. Some will sound strange to the reader, but it is the common experience that within a few months of joining the Navy the new entry uses them quite fluently, with a full knowledge of their meaning if not necessarily of their origin.

The newcomer soon learns that he stands no longer on the floor but on the 'deck', whilst the ceiling above becomes the 'deckhead'. No more is he surrounded by walls but by 'bulkheads', while going upstairs becomes going 'topsides' and going downstairs 'going below'. He never goes to bed – instead, he is asked to 'turn-in'; and when morning dawns he is requested to 'show a leg'. These expressions and hosts of others are not slang, but terms which have originated from the history of the Royal Navy itself.

When the human race began to travel by sea people naturally called many parts of the vessels in which they sailed after familiar objects on land. In other cases they likened things to, and named them after, parts of the human body, animals, domestic articles and the like. Still other words were taken from the foreign tongues heard by sailors in the course of their travels, were corrupted, and brought into the nautical vocabulary.

Consider the parts of a ship as an example. In nearly every case the expressions describing them are taken from the human being or an animal. Because the prows of early ships were often fashioned to resemble the head of a fierce animal or monster, we find this part named the ship's 'head' and the space around it the 'heads'. In sailing men-of-war lavatories were placed in this area and consequently the expression 'heads' still describes the ship's toilets, although their original situation has long since changed.

Having been blessed with a head, it is natural that a ship should have 'eyes', which are the two openings through which pass the ship's cables – in fact, the word 'hawse' is an old English word for 'throat'. From this comes the term 'hawse pipe', which aptly describes the channel through which the cable, 'hawser' or wire rope was passed, either for anchoring or towing. (Nowadays chain cable is generally used.) Similarly the 'bows' on either side of the ship's head are taken from another old English expression meaning 'shoulders'. Many other terms suggest their own origin, such as 'side', 'quarter', 'stern', etc.

Now we see how the names of animals have been brought into use:

Bull's eye. A light situated between two compartments so that it illuminates both.

Camel. A tank secured to a ship to provide it with extra buoyancy.

Cat or *Cat-o'-nine-tails.* An early instrument of punishment in the form of a whip composed of nine lengths of cod-line. Hence the expression 'no room to swing a cat', meaning to swing a cat-o'-nine-tails.

Crow's nest. A small shelter for the masthead look-out.

Dog-vane. A small tail of cloth attached in a suitable place on the windward side of a sailing vessel to show the direction of the wind.

Donkey. Any mechanical device for saving manual labour on board a ship. A 'donkey engine' is used for working small winches, and the sailmaker's 'donkey' is his sewing machine.

Other expressions involving the use of animals' names include: 'lizards' – canvas-covered wire pendants used for securing a ship's small boats; 'staghorns' – strong posts on a jetty which are used for securing small ships alongside, or for the securing of halliards in yachts; 'to mouse' – to secure a hook so as to prevent it from unhooking (this is done by tying spun yarn across the open end of the hook, thus transforming its shape into something akin to a mouse-hole); 'to worm' – to fill the grooves round a rope or cable by winding spun yarn or twine around them in wormlike fashion.

When one refers to a ship's rigging almost everything is named after a horse's harness. The word 'horse' itself is given to a curved bar of metal which is still found in certain types of small yacht. To this bar is attached a pulley block which controls the movement of the yacht's halliards, etc. Other terms in use which fall into this category include:

Bitts. These are strong wooden posts, still found in the bigger types of sailing vessels such as schooners and clippers. When the vessel is alongside a jetty the ropes from the 'staghorns' ashore are secured around the 'bitts'. They thus perform a similar function to the bit of a horse, namely a restraint on movement. All the early wooden men-of-war had their 'bitts' and many of these, from famous ships, now occupy places of honour in naval shore establishments.

Bridle. The cable that is taken from a ship's head when the vessel is being secured to a buoy out in mid-stream. In common with the bridle of a horse, it is a curb on movement.

Martingale. A short spar used to keep down any wooden projection from the ship's side, in exactly the same way as a martingale is used to snaffle or keep down the head of a horse.

Stirrup. Like the horseman's stirrup, a nautical 'stirrup' is a support. It holds the 'footropes' on the yards of a vessel. Yards are spars of wood fixed across the masts of sailing vessels to which are attached the sails. When sailors are working aloft on the yards they use the 'footropes' to move about in safety.

There are, of course, exceptions to these animal analogies, one being the term 'shrouds'. These were hemp (later wire) supports for the mast extending from the masthead to the ship's sides in the form of an inverted V. In the days when ropes were not of the strong quality of today, so many supports for the mast were required that the ship appeared to be wrapped in a shroud. The lower ends of the 'shrouds' were formerly secured to lanyards (later bottle-screws) attached to small platforms jutting out from the ship's sides. In early days these platforms were used by sailors when heaving the lead, a manual method still in use for finding the depth of water when nearing land. The 'lead' is a lead plummet which by skilful use can give the depth of water beneath a vessel.

Even in modern ship construction the word 'chain' survives – in the 'chain plates', which are strong steel plates riveted to the sides of a ship and serving the same purpose as in the days of sail, i.e. to provide a support for the ship's rigging and shrouds. Early ship constructors put a 'top' on the mast in which bowmen were stationed, and so the names 'topmast' and 'topsail' (the sail associated with the topmast) came into being. The top is no longer at the top of the mast, but the term remains. 'Fo'c'sle' is the contracted form of 'forecastle', a name which dates from very early days when castle-like wooden structures were erected in the bows and stern of men-of-war, from which positions soldiers hurled missiles at the enemy. The forecastle and the aftercastle (the castle in the stern) have gone, but the names still remain to describe two parts of a modern warship. For the purpose of cleaning, maintenance and general shipwork a warship is divided into parts and the forecastle (abbreviated FX) and aftercastle (abbreviated AX), or quarter-deck, form two of these divisions. There are others, and when each part assembles for the purpose of parade the process is known in the Royal Navy as 'Divisions'. This may sound a little illogical, but the origin is quite apparent, namely, the gathering together of people from all parts of the ship.

The following expressions, customs and names are also in common use today.

'*All my eye and Betty Martin*'. This is one way of describing something as nonsense. It originated in the following manner. A sailor once wandered into a church where a service was in progress and sat down next to a lady who was praying fervently but audibly. When asked afterwards how he had enjoyed the service, he remarked that it was 'all nonsense', for the lady who had been his companion had said it was 'All me eye and Betty Martin'. In point of fact, the lady had said in Latin 'A mihi, Beate Martin', meaning 'Oh help me, Blessed Martin'.

Andrew Miller or '*the Andrew*'. This means the Royal Navy. The term originated from a press gang officer named Andrew Miller, who seized so many men for naval service that he was said to own the Royal Navy.

Beam-ends. A ship is said to be in this position when she is lying over on her side, with her beams and decks perpendicular. The expression thus denotes a precarious position.

Bitter end. Formerly the length of a ship's cable inboard when the vessel was secured alongside a jetty. The term comes from the bitts to which the ends of the cable were secured.

To 'blow the gaff'. To divulge information. The origin of the phrase lies in the practice of a ship showing her identity to the world by hoisting her colours at the peak of her gaff, a short spar placed at an angle to the mast to which the ensign is hoisted when the vessel is at sea.

Blue-jacket. A name for a seaman. It originated from the short blue jacket that sailors used to wear.

To bolster. To support something. A bolster was a pad or cushion used at one time to prevent chafing between ropes.

'*To bone*'. To scrounge or steal. It originated in a boatswain of the name of Bone who was notorious for appropriating ship's stores and equipment.

'*By and large*'. A very common expression in use today meaning 'generally speaking' or 'under all conditions'. It originated from the sailing terms 'by the wind' (meaning sailing close-hauled, or as close to the wind as possible) and 'sailing large' (meaning running before the wind). In other words, the combination of the two expressions in the contracted form 'by and large' describes all possible conditions of sailing.

'*To clean*'. This expression means to change from one type of uniform into another and the words are followed by the name of the uniform in question. To a civilian it sounds strange when a ship's company is, for example, ordered to 'clean into overalls', which to a seaman simply means that he has to don an overall suit.

'*To crack on*'. To pretend. The expression comes from sailing days when, to give the enemy the impression that a vessel was exceptionally fast, more sails were set.

'*To cut and run*'. This means to escape; it arose from the early days of sail, when in an emergency the hemp cable attached to a ship's anchor was cut in order to get to sea quickly. When ships of the Spanish Armada were threatened by 'fireships' in Calais Roads they 'cut and ran', leaving their anchors on the sea-bed.

'Cut of his jib'. Descriptive of a person's appearance. In early days a ship was often identified by her 'jibs' – triangular sails borne in front of her foremast and varying in size and number. The phrase was extended to mean the human nose, which, like a jib, is the first part of its wearer to arrive.

Dead marine. A sailor's phrase for an empty bottle, which has done its duty and is ready to do it again.

'Devil to pay'. An expression meaning a difficult task ahead. Originally the phrase was 'the devil to pay and no pitch hot'. The 'devil' was the name given to the longest and most difficult seam to 'pay' or fill with tar. (Pay is from the French word 'poix', meaning pitch.) This seam was found near the piece of planking or strake situated next to the boat's keel, the strake being known as the 'garboard strake'. As the sides of a wooden boat were – and are still – made up of a series of curved wooden laths or strakes, the garboard strake is (apart from the keel itself) the one which is the deepest in the sea, and from this fact emerged the expression 'between the devil and the deep sea'.

Dhobying. The naval term for washing clothes. It is taken from the Indian word 'dhobi', meaning a washerman.

Fanny. The name given to any cylindrical tin container used in naval messes. The name arose in 1867 when a girl by the name of Fanny Adams was murdered and her body dismembered. Just about this time tinned meat was introduced into the Navy and the tins, when empty, were often used by sailors as containers. A button was discovered in one of these tins, and a wit of the day alleged that the button came from Fanny's pants. Thereafter, tin containers took on the nickname of 'fannies'.

Funeral ceremonies. At all funerals in which a naval guard of honour takes part it is the custom to reverse arms as an acknowledgement of the shame of killing. After the burial service three volleys are fired in the air above the grave. The idea behind this practice originally was to scare away any devils that might be about and might enter men's hearts when they were sad.

'Grog'. The mixture of one part rum and three parts water, so called after Admiral Vernon, who was nicknamed 'Old Grog' on account of a waterproof cloak made of grogram which he used to wear. Vernon was so alarmed by the heavy drinking of rum that in 1740 he ordered its dilution with water, a practice which was not popular among the sailors. The gratuitous issue of a 'tot' of Navy Rum, or 'Nelson's blood' as it was termed by many sailors ceased in 1970, on the grounds that its removal would make for more efficiency.

Launching ceremonies. Everyone is familiar with the launching ceremony that accompanies the christening of any new vessel, however humble. Nowadays it is customary to mark the appearance of a new ship by breaking over its bows a bottle of champagne. In Greek and

Roman times a similar ceremony was carried out, when a libation to the Gods was poured out. The Romans used water – water representing purity – and in naming their ship they always selected masculine names, whereas the Greeks favoured feminine titles. Today, of course, no matter what the name of a vessel, it is always referred to as 'she'.

Loggerheads. To be 'at loggerheads' is to be involved in a dispute. The expression came from the word 'logger-heat', a piece of iron on a long handle used in earlier days for melting pitch. This instrument was often used in the fights that arose out of disputes.

Make and mend. This means a holiday. Originally it was an opportunity for all hands to make and repair articles of clothing, and one half-day each week, usually on a Thursday, was set aside for this work.

Manning ship. On occasions of ceremony the ship's company man, or line up along, the ship's sides. In the days of sail the yards were manned, the men standing on the yards – not on the footropes – when a person of importance came on board, and also when he left the ship. When entering or leaving harbour the crew are fallen in inboard from the ship's side, facing outboard.

Master-at-arms. He is the most senior member of the ship's Regulating, or police, staff. The name arose from the old sea corporal and was first introduced into the navy in the reign of Charles I. The 'Master', as he is often called, had charge of all small arms on board and then, as now, had great authority. He is sometimes nicknamed the 'Jaunty', from the French word 'gendarme' or policeman. The Regulating staff in a naval establishment live together in a separate mess and at sea they are messed apart from the ship's company, even when the ship carries only one person from this branch of the navy. As a symbol of his authority the master-at-arms carries a sword on all ceremonial occasions – the only rating entitled to this privilege.

Moustaches. The wearing of moustaches alone is forbidden in the Royal Navy. They were banned by Queen Victoria on the death of her husband, the Prince Consort, as a token of respect. Since that time full sets, i.e. moustaches and beards, were grown, so as to distinguish sailors from soldiers, the latter for many years being more disposed to wearing moustaches. A sailor who wishes to grow a beard has first to request permission to do so from his Divisional Officer. If after a suitable period the Divisional Officer does not like the sailor's beard, the sailor will be ordered to remove it.

Muster by open list. This naval custom has now lapsed, but it used to be enforced once each quarter. Many naval personnel, some still serving, will know of the practice. The whole ship's company was assembled in the order their names appeared on the ship's pay ledger. Each person stepped before the CO and gave details regarding himself, his pay and allowances so that they could be verified. The object was to ensure that there were no 'fictitious' names on the list, a practice which occurred in the past when ships' captains were permitted to 'sign-on' members of the crew, often including fictitious names and by so doing, drawing the extra pay for themselves.

Neaters. Neat rum, i.e. without the addition of water. A daily tot of rum was one of the privileges of the Royal Navy, ashore or afloat. Formerly Chief and Petty Officers were allowed a tot of neat rum, junior ratings a tot of diluted rum, and officers a tot of rum only on very special occasions (see 'Splice the main brace'). If a rating elected to draw his rum ration he was noted on the ship's ledger as 'G' (or Grog); if not, he was marked 'T' (or Temperance), in which case a small money allowance was paid to him in lieu. The tot had to be drunk on the day of issue, and the accumulation of tots for the purpose of bottling the rum was strictly forbidden though this practice did occur.

'*Out pipes*'. An order which means 'Cease smoking' – the word 'pipe' in this connection meaning the tobacco pipe, not the boatswain's pipe. In time gone by a place on the upper deck of warships was set aside for the purpose of smoking, where groups of sailors during their 'stand-easy' periods could be seen busily puffing away over a tub of water. The latter was a precaution against fire, so necessary in wooden vessels.

Pipes and piping. In ancient Greek and Roman times a pipe or flute was used to keep the galley slaves in time when pulling on their oars. Later the pipe became a badge of office and a mark of high rank, and the Lord High Admiral carried a silver whistle on a chain round his neck. Today the boatswain's pipe (or 'call') is used for salutes and to 'pipe' orders. The expression 'to pipe' describes the sound made by the pipe, together with the spoken order which may qualify it. Some pipes are orders in themselves and do not require any verbal explanation, such as 'Pipe down', which denotes the order to the ship's company to 'turn in'. During this period it is the custom not to mark the time by the ship's bell, so as to avoid disturbing those who are asleep. The sound of the boatswain's call is rather similar to the sound of a person whistling, and it is to avoid confusion with piped orders that whistling is forbidden on board HM ships.

PIPING THE SIDE. This is a special pipe to herald the arrival on board of the Captain or senior naval officers. The custom originated in early days when one had to make use of a jumping ladder, hanging vertically from the ship's side, in order to climb on board a ship lying out in mid-stream. Captains of ships did not use this ladder, but instead were hoisted aboard in a boatswain's chain – a wooden seat operated by a system of pulleys. The sound of the boatswain's pipe regulated the movement of this chair, commencing with low notes which were gradually raised in pitch to signal the hoisting process and finally lowered again to regulate the descent of the chair to the deck of the ship. This practice has ceased, but the piping ceremony, with its wail of low and high notes, is still used to herald the arrival of important visitors.

Port and starboard. The port side of a ship is the left-hand side looking towards its bows, and the starboard side is the right-hand side. Originally the port side was known as the 'larboard' side, a name which came either from 'lee-board', a large, flat wooden structure or board lowered over the lee side (the side sheltered from the wind) to prevent a sailing vessel from being forced sideways in the water by the wind; or from 'load-board', the side of a vessel used for loading cargo. Whether 'lee-board' or 'load-board' gives the true origin is open to argument, but regarding 'starboard' there is no doubt, for this term originated in 'steer-board', a large, flat steering oar which acted as a ship's rudder and was operated from a position on the right-hand side of the vessel.

Pusser. The naval term for the Purser (later, Paymaster) or the Supply Officer, who is today responsible for the pay, food and clothing of the ship's company. Anything which comes from his department, whether it be peas or pyjamas, is referred to as 'belonging to the pusser'. It is interesting to note that Service knives (or, more aptly, 'pusser's knives') used as cutlery have rounded ends instead of pointed ones. At one time, however, they had points, and were often used as weapons in violent quarrels.

Rabbit. Any article made on board or converted from Service stores to private use is known as a 'rabbit'.

Saluting. This custom originated in the days when a sailor wore his hair in a forelock. On approaching an officer, he touched his forelock to show that he had no weapon in his hand.

SALUTING THE QUARTER-DECK. The quarter-deck of a warship is a hallowed place. It is situated towards the ship's stern or her quarters, and its approaches are often marked by a brass strip fixed on the deck itself. Anyone crossing the quarter-deck of a warship salutes. Even naval shore establishments have their quarter-decks and when boys were enlisted they were obliged to run across this space as a mark of respect. The origin of the reverence shown is obscure. Some authorities say it originated in the days when a crucifix or a religious statue was displayed on the quarter-deck. Others state that the custom is derived from the early practice of junior officers uncovering their heads on the quarter-deck when addressing senior officers. Whatever the true origin may be, the practice is universal throughout the Royal Navy.

GUN SALUTES. When under way and firing a gun salute a ship's head is pointed in the same direction as that of the ship saluted. This is a mark of respect. Originally shot was used, but this waste of ammunition was in time prohibited and special saluting guns were brought into use. Ancient superstition has it that the number of shots fired should be odd, and it was recorded in 1685 that 'the odd number in ways of saluting is so observable that, whenever guns be given otherwise, it is taken for granted that either the Captain, Master or Master Gunner is dead in voyage.'

Saluting guns are mounted on both sides of the ship and the guns are fired from alternate sides, beginning with a starboard gun.

'*Show a leg*'. An expression used when calling the hands in the morning. It dates from the times when women were carried in men-of-war. They were allowed an extra half-hour in their hammocks and the proof of entitlement was to 'show a leg', proving thereby that its owner was really a female and not some lazy sailor.

Skylark. A term now used to denote a prank. In the Royal Navy there is an order 'Hands to dance and skylark', which signifies that the ship's company may relax. The word 'lark' is said to be a corruption of an Anglo-Saxon word 'lac', meaning to play – in fact, in certain parts of Northern England to this very day a man who is out of work is described as 'laking' or playing. In the early days of the Royal Navy the word 'skylark' was used to describe the practice of young sailors who came down from the yards by sliding down the stays (the supports for the mast).

Slops. The name used for articles of clothing which can be purchased from the clothing store on board. The name came from ashore, where a shop which sold ready-made or second-hand clothes was once known as a 'slop shop'.

'Son-of-a-gun'. An expression still sometimes used to describe a sailor's son, the identity of the father being uncertain. The phrase originated in the days when children were sometimes born aboard men-of-war – quite often between a ship's guns. An old naval saying described such a child as 'begotten in the galley and born under a gun; every hair a rope yarn, every tooth a marline spike, every finger a fish-hook, and in his blood good Stockholm tar'.

'*Splice the main brace*'. This expression came from the days of sail, when sailors who performed this rather onerous job were rewarded with an extra tot of rum. (The main brace was one of the more important ropes in a ship.) Although the free issue of rum has now been abolished, provision is still made for an issue of a tot of rum, or other spirits or even cans of beer, when the occasion warrants, e.g. a Royal review of the Fleet, Royal Wedding and etc.

Sword. When an officer is tried by court-martial and found guilty, his sword is placed on a table in the court-martial room so that the point is towards him; if he is found not guilty, the hilt of the sword is directed towards him. This practice arose from the old custom of an executioner preceding a prisoner after sentence had been passed. If the executioner carried his axe with the blade turned downwards or toward the prisoner, it was a signal to the awaiting crowds that the prisoner had received the death sentence; but if the axe blade was turned upwards or away from him, the people knew that the prisoner's life had been spared.

Tar. A sailor. The name is derived from the old custom of tarring sailors' clothing to render it waterproof.

Tattooing. This practice appears to have originated in Europe as a mark of identification for the dead and wounded on the field of battle. It is still quite a common practice in the Navy today, though for a different purpose; but at no time does it receive any official encouragement.

Ticklers. This is the naval name for Service tobacco issued by the Supply Officer. As a duty-free concession every sailor afloat is allowed, under certain conditions, 300 cigarettes or the equivalent in pipe tobacco once each month, at duty-free prices and issued in packets marked 'RN'. Before it was issued in packet form, all duty-free naval tobacco, whether for pipes or cigarettes, was issued in tins. The first appearance of naval tobacco in tins was in the year 1908, and at the same time a first issue of jam in tins also made its appearance. The jam was produced by a firm named Tickler and the sailor, so alive to nicknames, transferred the name to the cigarette issue. Ever since then Service tobacco has been known as 'ticklers', while jam is still 'jam'!

Time. Time, apart from the 'silent hours' (see 'Pipes and piping'), is denoted by the striking of the ship's bell every half-hour. For convenience in spells of duty the day is split into 'watches'. The 'morning' watch is from 4 a.m. to 8 a.m., and this is followed by the 'forenoon' watch, which ceases at noon. From noon to 4 p.m. is called the 'afternoon' watch, and the period from 4 p.m. to 8 p.m. is divided into what are called 'dog watches' (originally watches that were 'docked' or shortened). From 4 p.m. to 6 p.m. is known as the 'first dog watch' and from 6 p.m. to 8 p.m. is the 'last dog watch'. The four hours from 8 p.m. to midnight comprise the 'first' watch, and the period following, the most unpopular of all, is the 'middle' watch, which lasts until 4 a.m., when the whole sequence recommences. The first half-hour of each watch is denoted by one ring on the ship's bell, and so on up to a maximum of eight bells for each watch with the exception of the dog watches, for which the maximum is four bells; 8 p.m., however, is eight bells. The purpose of dividing the period from 4 p.m. to 8 p.m. into two small watches is to provide an odd number of watches in a 24-hour period so that each sailor will keep different watches on successive days. It is not sufficient to describe the time as, for example, 'five bells'; one must specify also the watch in question. For instance, five bells in the forenoon watch would mean 10.30 a.m., whereas four bells in the first watch would mean 10.00 p.m.

A ship's bell is used also in fog, when the rapid ringing at one-minute intervals denotes the presence of a vessel at anchor. On New Year's Eve, at midnight, the youngest sailor in a ship has the honour of ringing the bell 16 times – 8 strokes to signify the end of the old year and 8 for good measure, to welcome the new.

'Toe the line'. To accept a rule or a custom. The expression arose from a very early naval practice, when sailors were lined up for inspection. To ensure that the lines were straight, the pitch seams between the deck plankings were used as a guide, and then the expression was 'toe the pitch'.

Uniform. Many picturesque stories are heard regarding the origin of various articles of a sailor's uniform. Unfortunately, the majority of them are untrue; and in nearly every case the origin has a practical background and not a romantic one. The bell-bottomed trousers, for instance, are for convenience when scrubbing decks, as they can be rolled up easily. The close-fitting jumper is again practical, for it offers little resistance to the wind and has no loose pieces or pockets to catch in the rigging. The sailor's collar was worn originally to prevent his pigtail, so popular at one period, from soiling his jumper; and the three rows of white tape which frame his collar are for pure decoration and having nothing to do with Nelson's three glorious victories, as is often supposed. Nor has the length of black silk round a sailor's collar anything to do with mourning for Nelson. Its original use was, again, a practical one, namely as a sweat rag: tied around the forehead in the heat of action, it prevented beads of perspiration from trickling down into the eyes.

Wardroom. A naval officers' mess. Originally the word was 'wardrobe' – a piece of furniture carried on board in which valuable articles were stored. Officers often sought privacy in its vicinity, and in the course of time the term was corrupted to its present form.

Washout. Something useless or finished with. This originated before the days of signal pads, when messages were taken down on a slate. After the signal had been noted, the message was rubbed or washed off the slate, since it was no longer of any significance.

Wedding garland. A garland of evergreen hoisted aloft to celebrate the marriage of someone on board, a practice which had its origin in the days when women were allowed on board HM ships.

At the beginning of this chapter it was stated that the customs, names and expressions mentioned are but a small part of those in common use. Indeed, there are many more, some of which over the years have become part and parcel of the English language. The modern sailor, like his earlier counterpart, is never at a loss to invent new names and phrases which give greater force and richness to his conversation, and it seems inevitable that some of the sayings and expressions of modern sailors will find their way into the English language and enrich it in the same manner as those of the past have done.

CHAPTER ELEVEN

Modern British Warships

Warships are usually classified under 'type' and 'class'. The term 'type' is used to distinguish between warships built for different purposes such as assault ships and guided missile destroyers.

The title 'class' is used to differentiate between ships which, although of the same type and thus having many similarities, are employed in slightly different rôles, e.g. the *Rothesay* Class frigate, which is primarily an anti-submarine warship and the *Tribal* Class which has a general purpose rôle. Additionally, as a means of identification of both type and class but not the specific name of a warship, there is a type of naval shorthand by which people with knowledge of the key can easily be made aware of the particular type and rôle. This shorthand is a combination of three or four letters of the alphabet which are internationally accepted to indicate a certain type of warship. In this code, the Royal Navy's assault ships, HMS *Intrepid* and HMS *Fearless*, are signified by the letters LPD, where the letter D represents the word Dock. Both these vessels have a dock in their open sterns through which landing craft can be floated out. With this same agreed shorthand, guided missile destroyers are represented by the letters DDG and nuclear submarines which are armed with ballistic missiles (our *Polaris* class) are referred to by the letters SSBN, the B and the N standing for ballistic and nuclear, respectively. If the submarine is nuclear-propelled but is armed with conventional torpedoes, the designation is SSN, and a propelled, attack conventional submarine carries the signification SSK.

Submarine

The essential feature of a submarine is the long, cigar-shaped hull which contains all the machinery and living quarters. On each side of this hull is a blister construction containing ballast tanks. The superstructure amidships is the bridge and conning tower which gives access to the main hatch. Periscopes and the 'snort' apparatus lead up from the control room. Torpedo tubes are fitted in the bows and stern, and propulsive power is provided either by means of a nuclear reactor, as in the case of the *Polaris* and *Fleet* classes, or by diesel engines when on the surface and electric motors when submerged for the conventional submarine.

The *Polaris* Class consists of four 7000-ton displacement vessels, HMS *Repulse*, HMS *Renown*, HMS *Revenge* and HMS *Resolution*. They each carry 16 *Polaris* missiles and their primary role is as a strategic nuclear deterrent.

The keel of the *Renown* was laid down in June 1964, followed by the keel of the *Revenge* in 1965 and by March 1968, all four had been launched. Their construction had involved a coordinated effort by hundreds of British and American firms at a total cost of £350 million for the four vessels. Each is some 425 ft in length and has a beam of 33ft, with good living accommodation and amenities for 13 officers and 130 ratings which make up the complement of each *Polaris* submarine. They have high underwater speeds and despite their large dimensions, they handle easily and quietly and so are able to operate in the oceans of the world with little fear of detection.

The first of the *Fleet* or *Valiant* Class of submarines, was the Royal Navy's first nuclear submarine, HMS *Dreadnought*. This class which now comprises the *Dreadnought*, HMS *Valiant*, HMS *Warspite*, HMS *Churchill*, HMS *Conqueror*, HMS *Courageous*, HMS *Swiftsure*, HMS *Sceptre*, HMS *Sovereign*, HMS *Superb*, HMS *Spartan*, HMS *Splendid*, and HMS *Trafalgar* (and two others on order) are all nuclear-propelled but carry conventional torpedoes as armament.

Conventially powered submarines the *Oberon* and *Porpoise* classes are known as Patrol Submarines. Although their endurance underwater is not as great as their larger nuclear sisters, they are silent and very difficult to detect, and more suited to operations in shallow water

In July 1971, the Queen authorised the issue to submariners of a distinctive badge to indicate the special rôle played by this increasingly important branch of the Royal Navy. This badge is a metal brooch which shows two dolphins supporting a crown over a fouled anchor and is worn on the left breast of uniform. To qualify for this brooch every submariner must complete satisfactorily three different parts of the submarine training course, theory, his specialist application to work in the submarine and practical work at sea.

Assault Ships

Two assault ships, the *Fearless* and the *Intrepid* are now in service with the Fleet. They are the most versatile vessels yet built for amphibious warfare. Each is fitted out as a Naval Assault Group/Brigade HQ from which naval and military personnel, working in close cooperation, can mount and control an amphibious operation. They can transport a military force and its supporting armour in various types of landing craft which are floated off from the ship's open stern. Additionally, the ships can operate a flight of assault helicopters and are armed with Seacat guided missilesand 40 mm guns for self defence. Such missiles are used for close range anti-aircraft armament but they can also be employed in a surface-to-surface rôle. Their guidance is radio-controlled and they are propelled by solid fuel rocket motors.

Anti-Submarine Carriers

The first of three anti-submarine carriers, HMS *Invincible*, was launched in 1977. It operates Sea Harrier V/STOL aircraft and Sea King anti-submarine helicopters. The Sea Harrier is a product of Hawker Siddeley Aircraft Ltd., and can be used in a strike/fighter/or reconnaissance rôle. Each ship displaces around 20 000 tons and has a complement of about 1000 officers and men. The new cruisers represent a further step in the increasing development of gas-turbine propulsion in warships. *Invincible*'s sisters are named *Illustrious* and *Ark Royal* – the latter name so famous as an aircraft-carrier in the Second World War and more recently as the carrier of 43 000 tons which has now been scrapped. HMS *Hermes,* originally completed in 1959 as a fixed wing aircraft carrier of around 20 000 tons displacement. (other ships of her class were *Albion, Centaur* and *Bulwark,* all of which were later converted to Commando carriers) is also now in service as an anti-submarine carrier.

Guided Missile Destroyers

Originally, there were seven guided missile destroyers of the County Class, the first of which, HMS *Devonshire*, has now been disposed of. She was planned as a 5000-ton destroyer, but finally she displaced nearer 6000 tons – in fact, because of her size, many naval writers refer to her as a cruiser rather than a destroyer. This Class carries Seacat and Seaslug missile systems. The Seacat has been mentioned already as a close-range anti-aircraft missile which can also be used in a surface-to-surface rôle. In contrast, the Seaslug is a medium-range ship-to-air missile. It has four propellant boosters which jettison after they have 'burnt out'. Four of the class were fitted with two modern 4.5-inch gun turrets, one forward and the other aft, whilst the remainder sacrificed one of the turrets in favour of a missile mounting for the French Exocet missile, a surface-to-surface missile which achieves high lethality by flying at very low altitudes.

Another guided missile destroyer is HMS *Bristol*, sometimes referred to as a Type 82, although she is the only one of her class. She has a greater displacement than her *County* Class sister ships but is slightly shorter in length. She is also armed with a 4.5-inch gun but uses the Sea dart missile system and the Ikara anti-submarine weapon. The Seadart is a ship-to-air medium-range missile and is propelled by a ramjet, it is smaller and lighter than the Seaslug and thus can be installed in small ships. The Ikara is an anti-submarine missile developed by the Royal Australian Navy. It is designed to deliver homing torpedoes at long range and with high accuracy. Propelled by a rocket motor, Ikara is an all-weather rapid reaction system.

The steam turbine propulsion systems of the guided missile destroyers are backed up by gas-turbine boost machinery. By the use of gas turbines extra speed can be obtained at very short notice.

A newer class of destroyers is the *Sheffield* Class. They displace 3500 tons, are 410 ft long and have a beam of 47 ft. They are powered by Rolls-Royce Olympus and Tyne gas-turbines and their armament includes a rapid-fire 4.5-inch gun, anti-submarine torpedo tubes and the Sea Dart missile system. Whereas the County Class carries a Wessex anti-submarine helicopter, the Sheffield class uses the Lynx. This is a high-speed multi-purpose helicopter which is highly effective for anti-submarine attack, surface search and strike against surface vessels. In commission at the present time are HMS *Sheffield,* HMS *Birmingham,* HMS *Newcastle*, HMS *Glasgow*, HMS *Coventry*, HMS *Cardiff* and HMS *Exeter*. HMS *Southampton* is undergoing trials. A further three, HMS *Liverpool* HMS *Nottingham* and HMS *Manchester* are under construction.

Frigates

The primary function of frigates is to protect task groups and convoys against enemy aircraft and submarines, and the types of frigates in service are dictated by their specific rôles, namely, as an anti-aircraft frigate, anti-submarine or a general purpose frigate, the latter being provided with armament and electronic equipment to cover all rôles.

The *Amazon* Class, sometimes referred to as Type 21, first appeared in 1974 and now consists of eight warships each of around 2500 tons and carrying a 4.5-inch gun and Sea Cat and Exocet missile systems. A later modernised version is to carry the Sea Wolf system.Ships of this class have names which commence with the same initial letter A and are powered by Rolls-Olympus and Tyne gas-turbines. Like the *Sheffield* Class of guided missile destroyers, they also carry a Lynx helicopter.

The most numerous frigates in service are those of the *Leander* Class. Their armament consists of a triple-barrelled anti-submarine mortar, the Seacat guided missile system, twin 4.5-inch guns and originally a Wasp helicopter, but this is now being replaced by the Lynx. The main propulsion machinery consists of two sets of steam turbines developing 30 000 horse power and giving speeds in excess of 30 knots. They are among the finest seakeeping ships ever possessed by the Royal Navy. The namesake of this class HMS *Leander* together with her sister ships, HMS *Ajax*, HMS *Galatea*, HMS *Naiad*, HMS *Aurora* and HMS *Euryalus* have been fitted to operate the Ikara anti-submarine weapon system whilst another eight vessels (HMS *Phoebe*, HMS *Cleopatra*, HMS *Minerva*, HMS *Juno*, HMS *Penelope*, HMS *Argonaut*, HMS *Danae* and HMS *Sirius*) have been adapted to fit the Exocet missile.

A class of frigates which have a general purpose rôle are the *Tribal* Class of which seven were HMS *Ashanti*, HMS *Eskimo*, HMS *Gurkha*, HMS *Mohawk*, HMS *Nubian*, HMS *Tartar* and HMS *Zulu*. They each displace around 2500 tons, carry two 4.5-inch guns, a triple-barrelled anti-submarine mortar and carry a Wasp helicopter. Now somewhat elderly, they have been withdrawn from service but may be preserved and used again should this be necessary.

The *Salisbury* Class Frigate which consisted originally of HMS *Salisbury* and HMS *Lincoln* were fitted for the direction of carrier aircraft, have now been transferred to the reserve.

The anti-submarine frigate is the primary rôle of the *Rothesay* Class, or Type 12's. They are made up of 10 warships each of around 2200 tons displacement, with a complement of 250 and are armed with two 4.5-inch guns, a triple-barrelled anti-submarine mortar and a Seacat missile system. Although they were built between 1960–61, their manoeuvrability, performance and seakeeping qualities, particularly at high speed, has made them very popular warships.

A somewhat larger anti-submarine frigate, of around 4000 tons displacement which puts it on a par with the guided missile destroyer, is coming into the fleet. This is known as the *Broadsword* Class, or Type 22's. At the time of writing ten are planned, the first, HMS *Broadsword* is to be followed by HMS *Brilliant*, HMS *Battleaxe* and HMS *Brazen* whilst two others are on order. Their armament will consist of two missile systems, Sea Wolf and Exocet, anti-submarine torpedoes and two Lynx multi-purpose helicopters.

Mine Counter-Measures Vessels

In May 1945, after the end of the war in Europe, an international board was set up under the presidency of a British admiral to formulate plans for minesweeping of the ocean trade routes. Captured and surrendered charts from many sources gave details of all enemy minefields and these revealed that in the waters of north-west Europe (the Baltic excluded), the Germans had laid around 125 000 mines and almost 100 000 in the Mediterranean. The British, too, had laid in the same areas a total of about 250 000. Only a small percentage of these had been swept and as the mines which remained were of different types, magnetic, acoustic and pressure operated, clearance of them even on an international scale did produce difficulties.

Member states of the Central Mine Clearance Board included France, Britain, Russia and the United States and they divided the areas to be cleared into four main zones which in turn were sub-divided into smaller areas. This brought into the scheme other countries, so that in what was called the East Atlantic Zone or Eastlanzon, besides the UK and the USA, France, Belgium, Denmark, Holland, Norway and the USSR all shared in the mine clearance.

Another important zone was the Mediterranean where the UK had a major share in the mine clearance. Indeed, when all affected zones were taken into account, the UK had by far the largest proportion of mine clearance work and employed over 500 vessels in the task. British minesweepers were also loaned to other countries which did not have suitable vessels, and although a time limit had been set for the world-wide clearance of all zones, it became clear that the original date had to be extended because the effective life of the magnetic mine proved to be longer than anticipated, sometimes up to 12 years, depending upon the state of its batteries.

In 1960, by means of a new type of detection device, it became possible for mines and other objects to be detected with far greater accuracy and range than ever before. These new mine hunting Sonar sets were tested by the Royal Navy and the United States Navy and as these proved so successful, they were installed in existing and new vessels employed in this work. So, in consequence a new breed of warships appeared in what are now known as minehunters which, together with minesweepers, have the generic name of mine countermeasure vessels or in the new nautical shorthand, MCMV's.

Currently, there are some 35 MCM vessels and between them they can deal with all types of mines. They are called the '*TON*' Class because the majority of their names end with this suffix. Usually, so as to obviate the effects of magnetic mines that are to be swept, mine countermeasures vessels are made of wood (usually mahogany) and where metal has to be used, a non-magnetic variety is employed.

Experimenting has proceeded with the use of glass-reinforced plastics for hull construction and the first MCMV of this type HMS *Wilton*, was successful and a new class of MCMV's called the *Hunt* Class, each constructed of glass reinforced plastics, is being built.

The first of these, HMS *Brecon*, was introduced to the Fleet recently and she is to be followed by HMS *Ledbury*.

The above are the main types of warships in use but there are many other types which can only be listed briefly here. These include patrol craft and offshore protection vessels, which are used to safeguard British offshore interests in the North Sea oil and gas fields and in protection of our fishery interests; survey ships, which carry out hydrographic and oceanographic surveys so necessary if the Admiralty Hydrographic Department is to keep its charts accurate: landing ships and craft of various types, used to put troops, tanks, motor transport and stores ashore in amphibious operations, boom defence vessels, which are used when laying harbour defences or as mooring ships and salvage vessels; hovercraft, which the Royal Navy employs in an experimental capacity and which could be used as fast patrol craft or in a mine countermeasures rôle; ships of the Royal Fleet Auxiliary, their supply vessels and oilers which replenish food, stores, ammunition and fuel to HM Ships at sea, and a host of other craft which all in their different ways contribute to the fighting efficiency of the Fleet.

CHAPTER TWELVE

Branches of the Royal Navy and Royal Marines

I ROYAL NAVAL AND ROYAL MARINE OFFICERS

There are three distinct types of careers for potential officers – short, medium or full which in the latter variety could mean employment in some specialisations to the age of 60 years. At the lower end of the scale, the entry age can vary from between 15 and 17 for those young men who have what is termed a 'reserved place' and to the age of 32 for those with degrees acceptable for entry to the Engineering and Instructor specialisations, and in the case of medical practitioners who wish to leave civilian medicine for the Navy, even up to the age of 39 years.

Naturally, the age of acceptability depends upon the specialisation intended and in turn the demanded educational standards. The former broadly consist of the Seaman officer, Engineering, Supply and Secretariat, Fleet Air Arm, Instructor, Medical, Dental and potential officers of the Royal Marines. There are detailed qualifications for admission to each of these specialisations, age limitations and career possibilities, and it is not intended in this publication to give them in full since these are available from most offices of the Naval Career's Service and in any event, full and current details of every specialisation can be had by writing to . . . The Royal Naval Careers Service, Officer Entry Section, Old Admiralty Buildings, Spring Gardens, London SW1A 2BE.

Short Service commissions

(a) *Seaman* Youths between the ages of 17 and 23 years can be accepted for SS Commissions of eight years with the option to leave after five years, provided they have 5 GCE 'O' level passes, which include English language, mathematics and a physics-based science. A gratuity is payable on leaving the service. Young men who are between the ages of 17 and 26 years can also be considered for a 3½-year SS Commission with an opportunity to extend this period.

(b) *Supply and Secretariat* This specialisation offers SS Commissions for youths between the ages of 17 and 23 years who have the same educational qualifications.

(c) *Fleet Air Arm* Candidates for Flying duties either as Pilots or Observers who have the same 'O' level qualifications and who are between the ages of 17 and 26 years, can be considered for SS Com-

missions of 12 years with the option to leave after eight years. Gratuities proportionate to the years of service are paid on leaving.
(d) *Royal Marines* Potential Royal Marine Officers who are between the ages of 17½ and 25 years can be considered for SS Commissions of four years' service with the opportunity to extend this to one of eight years. Educationally their 'O' levels must include passes in English languages and mathematics.
(e) *Engineering specialisation* Young Engineering graduates who are under the age of 32 years can be accepted for SS Commissions of eight years with the option to terminate their service after five years.

Medium Career Opportunities
A medium term career is one of 16 years service from the age of 21, at the end of which period a pension is paid for the remainder of the officer's life and a grant is given additionally, which amounts to a sum of money three times the amount of the pension awarded.
(a) *Engineering, Specialisation* 16-year pensionable careers are available for young men who are between 17 and 25 on entry and are in the possession of the following qualifications –
(i) five GCE passes, including two 'A' levels, normally at Grade C or above, in mathematics (pure and applied) and physics, and 'O' level pass in English language.
or (ii) an ONC in subjects appropriate to further mechanical or electrical specialisation: with a distinction or near-distinction in mathematics and credits in three other subjects; also a GCE 'O' level pass in English language.
(b) *Fleet Air Arm* Young men who are under the age of 26 years can be considered for Flying duties either as pilots or observers if they have five GCE passes at 'O' levels, three of which include English language, mathematics and a physics based Science.

Full Career Opportunities
Depending upon the specialisation and age of the potential naval officer, a full career may be started as such, or it may arise from a short service commission.
Seaman and Supply and Secretariat (a) Scholarship and Reserved Place Scheme (For Seaman only). Youths between the ages of 15 and 17 years who have five GCE 'O' level passes, including English language, mathematics and a physics-based science can be accepted for entry to the Naval College for a full career.
(b) Those who have five GCE Passes including English language, mathematics and a physics-based science (which can be waived in exceptional circumstances for the S & S specialisations and of the five passes, two are at 'A' levels, can be accepted for full naval careers.
(c) An offer of a place can be made to any student who is studying for

a degree at a University, Polytechnic or College of Technology, provided that at 'O' levels they secured passes in English language, mathematics and a physics-based science. The age limitations for this type of entry are from 17 to 24 on the year of graduation.
(d) Direct Graduate Entry. Full naval careers are offered to graduates of United Kingdom universities or others approved by the Ministry of Defence, provided a candidate gained 'O' level passes in English language, mathematics and a physics-based science. Age limitations are to a maximum of 25 years.
Engineering (a) Scholarship and Reserved Place scheme. Youths between the ages of 15 and 17 years who have five GCE 'O' level passes, including English language, mathematics and a physics-based science can be accepted into the naval college for a full career.
(b) Those who have five GCE passes, including 'A' level passes, normally at Grade C or above, in mathematics (pure and applied) and physics and an 'O' level pass in English language will also be accepted.
(c) An offer of a place can be made to any student who is studying for a degree at a University, Polytechnic or College of Technology provided the degree is in mechanical or electrical engineering or in a closely allied subject and that at 'O' levels a pass in English language was also achieved. Age limitations are from 17 to 24 on graduation.
(d) Direct Graduate Entry. Full naval careers are offered to Graduates of United Kingdom Universities or others approved by the Ministry of Defence provided that the degree is in mechanical, electrical or aeronautical engineering or a closely related subject. The age limitations for this entry are to a maximum of 26 years.
Instructor Officers He must have a degree or recognised professional qualification (HND, HNC in Engineering) or teaching qualifications, the main requirement being for men with science qualifications though a few arts graduates are entered annually. Candidates are taken from the age group 21–32 years and are given a short service commission of five years (with the option to terminate after three years). Opportunities are given for extensions of short service and for transfer to pensionable commissions.
Medical and Dental Officers There are three methods of entry for these specialisations –
(a) As a Medical and Dental Cadet. Preferably such young men are under the age of 25 years but the essential is that they must have passed their second MB (BDS for Dental officers) or a recognised equivalent.
(b) Pre-Registration Entry. This method of entry is for medical officers who have qualified and are about to take up their pre-registration appointments. Candidates who enter under these conditions are accepted to the age limit of 32 years.
(c) Qualified and Registered entrants. Entrants who are qualified medical and dental practitioners can be accepted for naval service provided

medical entrants are below the age of 39 years and dental entrants are under the age of 32 years.

Entrants are paid throughout their training prior to full registration and, additionally, those who enter under the Cadetship scheme, will receive an educational grant and their tuition fees will be paid provided, when qualified, they enter the Navy for a five years short service commission. If they withdraw from the Service before this period is completed, they will have to repay the grant and the fees so paid from public funds. Although the initial period of service is a five year short service commission, officers of both specialisations can transfer to pensionable commissions after completing the first year of their service.

Other Opportunities

Naval Chaplains There are other opportunities of service both in the Royal Navy and with the Royal Navy. In the first category are Naval Chaplains who serve in both shore establishments and at sea. They were regarded as civilians until about 100 years ago, when it was decided that they should have the status of commissioned officers without holding any rank. This arrangement is still in force today and, unlike Chaplains in the Army and Royal Air Force, Naval Chaplains wear no badges of rank even on their uniforms – if this is worn at all, for the choice between a civilian clergyman's attire and the prescribed uniform is left to the individual wearer. There are Church of England, Roman Catholic and Non-Conformist Chaplains, sometimes called Church of Scotland and Free Church Chaplains, serving in the Royal Navy. For members of other religions, commanding officers of ships and establishments ensure that every facility is given to officers and ratings to follow the denominations of their choice and, where practicable, to attend the services of that religion.

Candidates who wish to be considered for entry as Chaplains must be under the age of 35 years, be ordained and normally have had two or more years' experience in the work of a parish. Initially, they enter for a period of four years short service for which a gratuity is paid, and they may be considered for pensionable careers.

Constructor Officers The Royal Corps of Naval Constructors is a civilian body responsible for the design of HM ships and for the supervision of their construction wherever they are built. Members of this Corps are civil servants and are experts in naval architecture whilst some specialise in mechanical or electrical engineering. Although strictly civilians who work under quite different terms of service to uniformed naval officers, they do wear uniform when they are appointed to serve in one of HM Ships. There are two avenues of entry, namely, a schools entry and a university entry. The former is open to youths aged between 17½ and 19½ years who have good passes at 'A' levels in pure mathematics, applied mathematics and physics or pure and applied mathematics (as one paper), physics and chemistry.

The latter method of entry is for university graduates up to the age limit of 26 years who have first or upper second class honours degrees in naval architecture, mechanical science, electrical or mechanical engineering. Their appointments are governed by the Civil Service and are pensionable at the age of 60 years. Full details can be obtained from the following address – Civilian Management Specialists (2) Ministry of Defence, Empire Hotel, Bath, Avon.

Scientific Officers of the Ministry of Defence This is a large civilian organisation which works for the Royal Navy on research projects and is very much concerned with electronics and computers. Like officers of the Corps of Naval Constructors, they are civilians and are employed by the Civil Service. Normally on entry they have a first or second class honours degree in science subjects, although lesser qualifications are accepted for some of the work they undertake. The accepted upper age for entry is 32 years and a full career up to the age of 60 years is the usual term. Details of the career can be obtained from either of the following addresses: Ministry of Defence (PE) SPM 1B3, Savoy Hill, London WC2R OBX or Civil Service Commission, Alencon Link, Basingstoke, Hampshire.

Women's Royal Naval Services [WRNS]

WRNS Officers There are five methods of direct entry as a "Wren" Officer. One thing they all have in common is that entry as an officer is applicable to any young woman between the ages of 20½ and 26 years and once accepted, a Short Service Commission is granted for eight years with the option to leave the WRNS after five years and the right to apply for a pensionable commission. Those who leave after five or eight years receive a gratuity.

(a) Direct Entry (General) Any United Kingdom degree or Certificate of Education and GCE 'O' level passes in English language and mathematics.

(b) Direct Entry (Instructional Duties) A UK degree in mathematics, physics or engineering, preferably with honours, and GCE 'O' level passes in English language and mathematics

(c) Direct Entry (Secretarial) One year's full secretarial training, followed by at least two years in responsible posts, and five GCE 'O' level passes including English language and mathematics

(d) Direct Entry (Catering) An appropriate three-year course leading to a degree or HND and five GCE passes, including English language and mathematics

(c) Direct Entry (Physical Education) To have undergone a recognised full-time training leading to a degree or Qualified Teacher's Certificate in Physical Education. Also to have five GCE passes including English language and mathematics.

Nursing Sisters of the Queen Alexandra's Royal Naval Nursing Service Nursing Sisters who work in naval hospitals both at home and abroad and in certain naval shore establishments are accepted, provided they are under the age of 34 years on entry, for a five-year SS engagement with the right to extend this service for another three years and to apply for a pensionable commission. They have the right to leave the service after three years. Gratuities are payable for the SS commissions. Before entry to the QARNNS a young woman must be a State Registered Nurse with at least two years post-registration in a hospital

Quarters Officers These officers are accepted between the ages of 25 and 37 years under the same conditions for both SS Commissions and pensionable careers as Nursing sisters. On entry they must be in the possession of a Diploma of the Hotel Catering and Institutional Management, or a Domestic Science Certificate, and at least one year's post-qualifying experience.

II RATINGS AND OTHER RANKS

1. Royal Navy

Missile firing, submarine hunting, manning sophisticated communications systems, diving, operating radar, plotting exercises, steering the ship or driving power boats – these are some of the specialised jobs open to young men who enter the Operations Branch of the Royal Navy.

The expertise provided by this Branch covers such a wide range of duties that it is divided into two groups – the Seaman Branch and the Communications Branch. The former provides the skills required to man the various weapon systems and to 'fight the ship' which, among other things, includes an expert knowledge of seamanship. The latter, as its name implies, contains men who have a expert knowledge of a wide range of communications systems from teleprinters and radio telephony to radio and visual signalling. The operations group also embraces aspirants to the mechanical and electrical side of the service, future members of the Fleet Air Arm, the writer, cook, stores accountant and catering categories of the Royal Navy. What they all have in common is naval service and for this reason they all do some basic training at a naval shore establishment called HMS *Raleigh*, at Torpoint in Devon. Although it is called Her Majesty's Ship, it does not go to sea. It is just the Navy's way to get new entries of all categories and eventual specialisations accustomed to service in a ship. The age limitations for entry are from 16–33 years and those under the age of 17½ enter as a junior; otherwise as what is termed an ordinary rating. This initial period of common training is followed by further courses, some of which are held in HMS *Raleigh* but others elsewhere. In particular, future members of the Fleet Air Arm, namely naval airmen and air engineering mechanics of whatever sub-specialisation do their further training at the Royal Naval Air Station at Culdrose.

Generally speaking, the initial training for all new entrants to the Royal Navy is a common one, since the change from civilian life is quite different and there are many different customs and traditions to learn, all designed to make the change-over from a civilian life or occupation as easy as possible.

Young men are normally entered on a Long Service and Reserve Engagement i.e. nine years' service from the age of 18, or to the age of 27 if entered before reaching the age of 18. This is followed by service in the Reserve for three years. Some details of the sub-specialisations possible are given but in so doing, it must be emphasised that these are subject to change and should not be taken as 'gospel'. The Royal Navy, despite its rooted associations with the past, is a very progressive service and its regulations for entry, its categories and its specialisations are liable to change with changing circumstances; in other words, a check of career details from a Naval Careers Information Office will bring up-to-date information. At the time of writing, details are given of some of the sub-specialisations which follow the initial period of common training:

Electronic Warfare (EW) Concerned with the electronic equipment in operations rooms of ships mainly in the interception of 'enemy' transmissions.

Radar (R) Plotting positions of ships and aircraft.

Missile (M) Operation of ship's weapons

Sonar(S) Operating of sonar equipment used in the hunting of submarines

Diver (D) Mine disposal and mine clearance and in experimental diving

Mine Warfare (MW) Service in mine countermeasures vessels

Survey Recorder (SR) Compiling information for Admiralty Charts

Tactical Systems (Submarines) The operation of radar equipment, computers and plotting equipment. It should be noted that service in submarines entitles one to additional pay.

On completion of the basic training, men of the communications Group of the Operations Branch can sub-specialise for one of the following duties for which further training is given.

Radio Operator (Tactical) Concerned with message handling and procedures relating to the movements of ships.

Radio Operator (Submarines) Expert in the special communications systems used in conventional and nuclear submarines.

Radio Operator (General Radio) Mainly concerned with all types of radio equipment and with the handling of general signal traffic.

Marine Engineering Mechanic This specialisation is concerned with turbines, boilers, internal combustion engines and the machinery used in fuelling, refrigeration, the distillation of sea-water and the generation of a ship's electricity. Work could be in small ships such as minesweepers or in ships up to anti-submarine/commando carriers.

Weapon Engineering Mechanic The ships of today's navy are equipped with very sophisticated weapon systems and electronic equipment. Mechanics are concerned with the maintenance and operation of such equipment.

Weapon Engineering Mechanic (Radio) Ratings of this branch are concerned with radar, radio, television, automatic plotting and data handling systems as well as sonars.

Weapon Engineering Mechanic (Ordnance) Such ratings deal with ships' navigation systems, internal communications, gun mountings, missile launchers, explosives and the control of weapon and missile systems.

Writer He corresponds to the civilian office worker and plays a vital part in the administrative affairs of ships and naval establishments throughout the world. He may well be the only writer in a small ship or submarine but one of many writers on an Admiral's Staff in a NATO Command.

Stores Accountant He plays a most important rôle in the business of clothing officers and ratings, in the control of his stock and the custody of stores. Again, he may work alone in a small ship or with others in large warships and establishments. His initial training earns a Royal Society of Arts Certificate in Storekeeping.

Naval Airman He works on the flight deck of a carrier or a commando carrier or indeed ashore on naval airfields, inside hangars and control positions. He assists in directing the movements of aircraft so as to ensure their safety. He is of necessity trained in firefighting and all aspects of flight deck procedures. After his initial training he is then drafted to the Navy's largest helicopter station, HMS *Seahawk*, Culdrose, near Helston in Cornwall, where follows a 17-week course learning his duties.

Air Engineering Mechanic After his initial training in HMS *Raleigh* advice will be given in order to help the young air mechanic to select his trade from one of the following three options, mechanical, radio or weapons electrical. Whatever maybe the outcome, his next period of training occurs in HMS *Daedalus*, at Lee-on-Solent, Hampshire, not very far from the naval port of Portsmouth.

The mechanical side covers the aircraft's engines and airframes; radio, its communications, radar and sonar equipment and weapons electrical, the necessary maintenance of the aircraft's electrical system and armament.

Medical Assistant He is a member of a medical team trained for one of the three specialisations: naval medical assistant, submarine medical

assistant or commando medical assistant. After general experience he can specialise in one of the following: dental assistant, operating theatre assistant, venereologist assistant, State Enrolled Nurse and may qualify to transfer to the medical technician category.
Medical Technician He is trained in the highly specialised work of one of the following fields: physiotherapy, radiography, laboratory technical work, pharmacy, work in the dispensary or as a State Registered Nurse both in the general field or in mental health or indeed as a health inspector. In due course he would thus qualify for membership of the appropriate professional organisation. He could also be selected for nuclear health physics, for the City and Guilds of London Institute examination and where the technician has specialised in laboratory, for the Associate Membership of the Institute of Laboratory Technicians. As with so many of the specialisations in the Royal Navy, these opportunities provide a young man with getting qualifications which will be of immense value when he leaves the service for a second career in civilian life.
Artificer Apprentice He is a most highly skilled rating and thus his training is an apprenticeship – one taking some five years. He has to have a high standard of educational attainments on entry and be between certain age limits. Usually 'O' Levels or their equivalents in SCE examinations or in other recognised examinations, provided specified subjects have been passed, will gain exemption from the normal naval selection tests.

Whatever the sub-specialisation chosen, all artificers have a period of common training in order to gain operator certificates. This is undertaken in HMS *Fisgard*, near Torpoint in Cornwall. Thereafter the sub-specialisation follows, viz:
Weapon Engineering Training School At HMS *Collingwood*, near Fareham, Hampshire. This is the Royal Navy's largest shore establishment and where an artificer is trained as a weapon engineer artificer. This is followed by further development of specialisation in one of the following:
Weapon Engineering Artificer (Communications and Electronic Warfare) This concerns radio communications, cryptographic equipment, teleprinters electronic warfare, satellite communications, digital processing, sound reproduction equipment, closed circuit television and direction finding equipment.
Weapon Engineering Artificer (Action Data) concerned with surveillance, radar and radar displays, computer and action information systems, computer peripherals, digital processing, sonars and radio navigation aids.
Weapon Engineering Artificer (Weapon Data) concerned with weapon tracking, weapon computers, digital processing, missile control and guid-

ance systems, non-radio navigational aids, internal communications, torpedo control, compasses and air weapons.
Weapon Engineering Artificer (Ordnance Control) concerned with gun mountings, rocket launchers, missile launchers, torpedo systems, digital processing, bomb lifts, mine countermeasures, explosives ordnance and small arms
Weapon Engineering Artificer (Action Data and Communications) Submarine concerned with communications, cryptographic equipment, radar, sonars, Radio navigation aids, *Polaris* radio navigation aids, electronic warfare equipment and periscopes.
Weapon Engineering Artificer (Weapon Data and Ordnance Control) Submarines concerned with tactical weapons, fire control and computers, *Polaris* weapons their fire control and launching, non-radio navigation aids, submarine inertial navigation systems, internal communications and small arms.

On the purely propulsion side of the artificer specialisations there is the Marine Engineering Artificer School, HMS *Caledonia*, where again, after a period of common training in order to gain operator certificates sub-specialisation follows in either mechanical or electrical engineering viz:
Marine Engineering Artificer (Electrical) concerned with high-power electrical generation and distribution, all electrical equipment associated with a ships propulsion and auxiliary machinery, air conditioning, ventilation and other domestic services. Such sub-specialisation is carried out in HMS *Collingwood*, as also the training for the sub-specialisation of the
Marine Engineering Artificer (Mechanical) He is concerned with the propulsion machinery whether it be steam, gas turbine or nuclear power, also the ship's structure, boats and fittings and the mechanical side of all the domestic appliances within a warship.

On the Air Side there are three types of artificers and the initial common training is carried out in HMS *Daedalus*, the Fleet Air Arm Training Establishment at Lee-on-Solent, Nr Fareham, Hampshire. Further training there follows for one of the three sub-specialisations.
Aircraft Artificer He is concerned with the airframe structure of fixed wing aircraft and helicopters, their structure, engines, transmissions and all other mechanical systems.
Electrical Artificer (Air) His work embraces the power generation in an aircraft and its distribution, the flight control systems, weapon systems and of course the multitude of instruments carried in a modern plane and helicopter.
Radio Electrical Artificer (Air) As is implied in his title, his rôle is entirely concerned with the vital communication, navigation, sonar and radar systems of naval aircraft.

In general, artificers are very highly qualified personnel and as such, advancement up the promotion ladder is swift with opportunities for promotion to an officer for those who meet the educational requirements and who prove suitable candidates for even further qualifications. Once a rating becomes a second class artificer, he is entitled to full skilled membership of the appropriate trade union – if he wishes to join – a very useful qualification when it comes to leaving the Royal Navy and taking up a second career as a civilian.

Some categories or branches of the Royal Navy actually take their recruits from within the service. These are the Submarine Branch and the Navy's Police, known as the Regulating Branch.

Submarine Branch Ratings may volunteer or may be required for submarine service after their basic training. If they are recommended, accepted and are medically fit, they join HMS *Dolphin*, the Submarine Training School at Gosport, Hampshire (just across the water from Portsmouth). When they qualify, they may serve in any type of submarine for a period of five years and can volunteer for further submarine service afterwards. Submariners, who wear a special badge, receive extra pay but they are not necessarily supermen, rather dedicated experts who are very aware of their considerable responsibilities. A patrol may last only a few days or, as in a *Polaris* submarine, it may last months. There are nuclear-powered fleet submarines which can circumnavigate the world without surfacing, and conventional patrol submarines which are packed with complex machinery, computers and electronic gear. At present there are 31 submarines in service – four *Polaris* carrying nuclear missiles; eight nuclear-powered Fleet Submarines and 19 of the smaller diesel-electronic powered Patrol class. The Submarine Service is playing an increasingly important rôle and about 1000 new men are required annually to maintain it.

Regulating Branch This is a small branch for which ratings are selected on their powers of leadership and power of command. The branch has disciplinary and administrative duties. In a police rôle it is responsible for good order in ships and establishments, and for manning Naval Shore (Provost) Units in large naval towns. The branch deals also with mail, leave and travel. Welfare tasks are also part of the duties of this branch and indeed any problem concerned with the well-being of ships' companies. All major warships carry Regulating Staff and the senior Fleet Master-at-Arms – is responsible to the commanding officer for the discipline of his ship's company.

Premature Release and Re-engagement It would be foolish to expect that anyone who joins the Royal Navy really enjoys a life that is so different from the normal male civilian life. This fact is fully appreciated and anyone who feels soon after joining that such a life is 'not for him' is quite at liberty to leave. The rules governing their release are very straightforward, namely:

(a) If a person is under 18 on joining, he can apply to leave during his

first six months or before reaching the age of 18 years 3 months, whichever occurs first.
(b) If he is aged 18 and over on joining, then he can apply for release during his first three months of service.

There is another condition, namely, that those under 17½ on entry must give fourteen days' notice of their wishes and those over that age on entry are required to pay the sum of £20. This fee is simply a token sum as a contribution to the costs of their training already incurred by the Navy Department.

Re-engagement On the other hand, ratings serving on long service and Reserve engagements may volunteer to re-engage for a further five years and finally for a period of eight years, thereby serving for a total of 22 years from the age of 18. This qualifies them for a life pension with a terminal grant, or what is called in civilian life a 'golden handshake' of three times the annual total of the pension.

This is by no means the end of the story, for by the time a rating has completed his time for pension, he is around the age of 40 years, still quite a young man and probably by experience one who enjoys the Royal Navy and one whom the Service would like to retain. For these reasons, there are opportunities for selected ratings to sign for an additional five years to complete 27 years' service and for even a further period still of five years, making 32 in all. Such extensions of extra service are often referred to as 'fifth fives' or 'Sixth fives' and they enhance one's eventual pension, and as the terminal grant is currently three times whatever annual pension is awarded, a rating receives a correspondingly higher 'handshake'.

Prospects Whatever branch a rating joins he is obviously concerned with his prospects of advancement. If a person joins as a junior rating (i.e. under the age of 17½) he receives his first advancement to Ordinary Rate, automatically, at 17½. Thereafter advancement to Able Rate, subject to passing some tests, follows about 6 to 15 months later. The next step is to Leading Rate, the equivalent to army corporal. Again, there are certain tests but the average age of attaining leading rating is between 22 and 23 years of age. Then follows the rate of petty officer (like an army sergeant) and Chief Petty Officer (equivalent to an army sergeant-major). Depending upon ability, these advancements usually occur around the ages 26–28. The highest rating attainable in the Royal Navy is a Fleet Chief Petty Officer (equivalent to an army warrant officer) and anyone who achieves this rank is expected to serve to at least the age of 45 years.

Commissioned Rank For those who have higher ambitions and wish to become an officer, there is every opportunity for them to achieve this aim. Certain educational qualifications are necessary, the very minimum requirements being four 'O' Levels in certain subjects, but additionally the candidate must have shown in his duties certain qualities of which an ability to lead and to accept responsibility is very important. Then, provided the young rating is between 17½ and 23½, he is sent for officer training to the Britannia Royal Naval College at Dartmouth.

Another scheme offers commissions on what is termed the Special Duties List of officers. This type of commission allows a longer period of service as a rating and thus more time for study.

There are certain educational standards to be achieved and the age bracket on promotion is between 25–34, initially as a Sub Lieutenant with career prospects to the rank of Commander. The first scheme offers opportunities of promotion to the highest ranks in the Royal Navy but both schemes give a full career with higher pay and proportionately, higher pensions and terminal gratuities.

Service life does offer comradeship, security, medical care and for the married man, quarters. If on medical grounds service is cut short before completing agreed contracts, then gratuities or invaliding pensions are paid. Finally, to help those who are leaving the Navy in the normal way, there are courses at naval vocational training centres which assist a rating to prepare for a new career.

2 Royal Marines

About 1000 young men join the 'Royals' every year and as many more volunteer, but for one reason or another, fail to meet entry standards. To be accepted a young man must be of good character and conform with nationality regulations and pass a medical and selection test. Adults are accepted in the age group 17½–28 years or as a Junior or Junior Bugler between the ages of 16–17½. Provision is also made for some applicants between the ages of 16–28 years who fail to meet the normal medical requirements to enlist as cooks or clerks. Initial recruit training is conducted at the Commando Training centre at Lympstone and though it is broken by normal leave, it extends to 26 weeks for adult recruits (over 17 years of age on entry) and up to 35 weeks for younger men.

Adults start their training with a two-week period before moving on to more intensive training enabling them to take their place in a Commando Unit. Recruits under the age of 17 on entry, spend their first 13 weeks mastering the basics of weaponry and fieldcraft and their final 22 weeks training is similar to that taken by adult entries.

The ranks of the corps are of Army origin, the new recruit (except juniors) joining as a 'Marine' the equivalent of an army corporal. Thereafter advancements in rank follow the army pattern namely, corporal, sergeant, colour-sergeant, quarter-master sergeant and regimental sergeant major – who is a warrant officer.

Recruitment for the Royal Marines Band Service is somewhat different, for to join as a junior musician 2nd class, a young man must be between the ages of 16–17½ years and have some musical knowledge.

Naturally, it is an advantage if he can already play some musical instrument, but this is not essential. There are also opportunities for accepting trained musicians up to the age of 28 years. Training for all musicians and would-be musicians takes place at the Royal Marine School of Music at Deal, the army titles of ranks in the RM Band service being prefixed by the name Band e.g. Band Corporal, Band Sergeant and so on and the agreed periods of service are similar to those of the Navy.

Buglers and drummers form an integral part of the RM Ceremonial Marching Bands and they belong to the Bugle Branch of the Corps. Boys who have a musical aptitude are recruited as junior buglers between the ages of 16 and 17½ years and can advance to colour sergeant bugler and warrant officer bugler just as other members of the Band Service.

As for the 'Royal' who trains as a Commando, besides his infantry rôle, he selects a specialist duty taken from either what are termed 'General Duties' or the 'Technical Branch'.

By far the majority of marines are in the General Duties Branch and these cover a wide field, the marine receiving instruction in the rôle selected. The General Duties comprise: assault engineer, butcher, cinema operator, drill instructor, equipment repairer, groom, heavy weapons, landing craft crew, light aircraft pilot, air gunner and observer, parachutist, physical training instructor, platoon weapons, mountain and arctic warfare. Royal Marines Police and swimmer canoeist.

As for the Technical Branch, these marines are mainly tradesmen such as armourers, carpenters and joiners, drivers, illustrators, metalsmiths, printers, radio technicians and vehicle mechanics.

A few non-tradesmen are however included in this branch. These are buglers, clerks, cooks and signallers.

In all a truly versatile service, with many and varied opportunities both with the Royal Navy and, as a separate entity, in its commando rôle.

3 Women's Royal Naval Service

The WRNS came into existence in 1939, taking its name from the earlier organisation established during the First World War. Throughout the 1939–45 conflict this service performed valuable duties ashore, releasing men for service afloat. These included technical, administrative, domestic, secretarial, medical and communication duties. On 1st February 1949, the WRNS was established as a permanent service and an integral part of the Royal Navy. Their members are not subject to the Naval Discipline Act, but have their own code of conduct. Young women between the ages 17–28 years can be accepted for training, though with a parent's permission, a girl can be accepted for entry from the age of 16 years 9 months. An aptitude test is given to decide upon the most appropriate specialist training. The first five weeks is spent at the WRNS New Entry Establishment, HMS *Dauntless*, near Reading, Berkshire where the new recruits are introduced to naval life and are taught some of its customs and traditions. Very soon they learn that the 'floor' is in reality the 'deck' and if they go into Reading or anywhere away from HMS *Dauntless* they are going for a 'run ashore'. If, however, during the first two weeks a young woman decides that the naval life is not for her, she is quite free to leave. There are 18 different WRNS categories for which of course specialist training is given. They are:– air mechanic, radar, telephonist, cook, training support assistant, quarters assistant, weapon analyst, writer (general and pay), writer (shorthand), steward (officers), education assistant, motor transport driver, photographer, dental hygienist, dental surgery assistant, meteorological observer, radio observer and stores accountant.

Each different category wears its own individual badge, and promotion to Leading Wren, Petty Officer Wren, Chief Wren and Fleet Chief Wren is by a graded system of tests and the two highest ratings (Chief and Fleet Chief Wren), are promoted by selection. Until a Wren reaches the age.of 18 years, she has to live in WRNS quarters where her food and accommodation cost her relatively little but when she is over the age of 18, and her training is completed, she can live out or in naval parlance 'ashore' – that is if she so wishes.

A Wren serves on what is called a Notice Engagement. This entitles her to leave subject to a minimum of three years service after the completion of the specialist training or on compassionate reasons or marriage; in the latter case if she wishes, because a Wren can still continue to serve when she marries, in fact the authorities try to arrange that she serves near her husband which is possibly why many Wrens marry Service personnel. As with ratings, of both the Royal Navy and Royal Marines, there are excellent opportunities for promotion to the rank of officer and as with the regulations for their male counterparts, certain educational qualifications are required.

Naval Nurses and Quarters Assistant These categories are relatively new and are Notice Engagements (as for WRNS) but for a period of nine years with opportunities for further periods to 22 years with pension and terminal gratuity benefits. The early training is carried out at a naval hospital and details of duties etc, can be obtained from the Matron-in-Chief, QARNNS, First Avenue House, High Holborn, London WC1V 6HE.

4 Naval Reserves

The Royal Navy Reserve (RNR) plays a vital role in Britain's Naval Defence. It operates its own ships, the 10th Mine Counter-measures Squadron as part of NATO's defence force. Additionally, it supplies a source of essential skilled manpower to supplement the Royal Navy both ashore and afloat. In the Reserve, training is given for almost every naval rôle and this involves only a few hours weekly training, certain week-

ends and a period of 14 days during the summer months. The same is true for the Royal Marines Reserve and for the Women's Royal Naval Service Reserve. All training periods at week-ends and during the summer attract service pay and travelling expenses and an annual bounty is also given. Details of conditions of service, opportunities, etc., can be obtained from: RNR and WRNS Reserve, Commaner-in-Chief, Naval Home Command, Reserves Division (TA2R), HM Naval Base, Portsmouth. RM Reserve, Royal Marine HQ and Reserve Forces, Eastney Barracks, Eastney, Portsmouth. (For attention of GSO Reserves)
Royal Naval Auxiliary Service (RNXS) The RNXS is an unique volunteer organisation which trains in peacetime for vital tasks which members would undertake in time of war, thus relieving active service personnel for first-line duties. In the event of hostilities the Royal Navy would exercise control of merchant shipping, and the monitoring of all movements would be delegated to an organisation staffed by members of the RNR and RNXS. The RNXS is a civilian organisation, a non-combatant but uniformed service, whose members may opt for training in one of the specialist roles of seamanship, engineering, communications or operations, personnel training once weekly and occasionally at week-ends. Uniform is provided as well as travelling expenses, and a training allowance is given. Further information can be obtained from the following address:
The Area Naval Auxiliary Officer, RNXS, HMS *Vernon*, Portsmouth, PO1 3ER.

5 Associated Organisations
Royal Navy Auxiliary Service This is a volunteer organisation composed of local men and women who undergo spare-time training and who are responsible in time of war for many duties which would otherwise have to be undertaken by service personnel. Among these duties are spotting mines dropped from aircraft and plotting their positions. They would also form Port Parties – which, among other things, could provide the staff for Port Headquarters or Resident Naval Officers and Naval Officers-in-Charge of certain stations – thus augmenting the Naval Control Organisations.
Sea Cadet Corps This body is administered by the Navy League in conjunction with the Ministry of Defence. It is the oldest pre-service organisation for boys in Great Britain, dating from the Crimean War, 1854–6. Its aim is to give seamanlike training to boys under the age of 18, who intend to serve in the Royal and Merchant Navies, as well as providing the same training for boys who do not intend to follow a sea career but who could form a valuable reserve in war.
Civilian Support In addition to the uniformed personnel serving in HM ships and establishments, many civilians work for the Royal Navy. In a ship, running repairs and maintenance are the responsibility of the of-

ficers and ratings serving on board. Extensive repairs however, are undertaken by civilian craftsmen who work in a naval dockyard or naval base. The engineering judgements of ships' staffs are supplied with certain instruments which help them to decide what machinery on board needs repair or renewing on the next occasion a warship is due for its routine maintenance by dockyard personnel. A more recent aid to engineer officers in looking after their ships has been the provision of closed circuit under-water television equipment in the main Naval Bases. An expert can stay warm and dry on the jetty while getting a clear view of underwater defects on the television screen and the equipment can actually provide a clearer picture in conditions of poor visibility that can be seen by a diver. Television used in this manner has already proved its worth in saving several emergency dockings by warships.

CHAPTER THIRTEEN

The Future of the Royal Navy

This book has described something of the history and traditions of the Royal Navy, which, by virtue of its tasks and achievements, has become the most famous fighting force of all time – a Service which has weathered many changes and has already adapted itself to the new conditions imposed by the nuclear age. It is now entrusted with the responsibility for deploying four Polaris-equipped nuclear submarines as Great Britain's contribution to the large-range strategic deterrent forces of the Western Alliance. As always, the Royal Navy will have the responsibility of bringing conventional force to bear whenever and wherever necessary.

No matter what future political developments may bring, it is vital that the Sea lanes of the world remain free for the passage of our merchant shipping to carry the supplies of energy and raw materials that are essential to the economic survival of our western nations.

In the Queen's speech which opened the first Parliamentary session of her new Government in 1979, the first item stated that the 'Government will take steps to improve the security of the nation and to strengthen our contribution to the North Atlantic Alliance on which our defences are based.'

Apart from other measures the Government has taken a very important step towards this end by endorsing the NATO aim of increasing defence spending in real terms by 3% per year. 1979 saw the thirtieth anniversary of the North Atlantic Treaty Organisation and although the U.K. could allow itself some satisfaction at this achievement, it still faces the tremendous task of ensuring the effectiveness of NATO's forces in the light of the continued growth in Soviet military strength. If deterrence should fail NATO's strategy rests on the two pillars of forward defence and flexible response; this means ensuring that the NATO forces must have the capability to defend all its territories, must be able to respond to any level of aggression, and must be able to escalate the conflict appropiately if the enemy does not withdraw.

To play its part effectively, the Royal Navy must keep a careful balance between quality and quantity and between the capabilities of its various arms in an age of new, exciting and rapid scientific and technological development. To keep abreast of the times therefore is difficult because new inventions are expensive and take a long time to bring into operational service. The number of ships required must also be carefully planned in relation to the amount of money expected to be voted by

Parliament for their defence. Despite all these problems, the Royal Navy and the Royal Marines are maintaining a first rate capability on the surface, in the air and under the seas. The Fleet is provided with versatile, modern ships fitted with the most advanced equipment.

The advanced and complex weapon and ship systems now in the Fleet, require officers and men of the highest quality to operate and maintain them. Not all need have high scientific qualifications, but they must have a love of the sea and be willing to undergo the training necessary to understand and use modern technology to the best advantage. But life in the Navy will not be vastly different from what it has been in the past. It will still be a life of adventure, a life of travel, a life of service to one's country and one's fellow men. Naval personnel are Britain's ambassadors at large; the standard they set when they visit overseas ports helps to form the image of this country which remains in the minds of their hosts. Again, a deep impression is made when ships of the Fleet are called upon, as they often are, to render help to ships in distress and to countries devastated by flood or earthquake.

No one would expect to make his fortune in the Navy: the days of Sir Francis Drake and the Spanish treasure galleons have gone; but the Royal Navy does provide good pay as well as things which money cannot buy, such as a healthy life, a life of comradeship and, above all, a happy and challenging career in the service of one's Country.

Despite all the scientific developments of the nuclear age, the maze of electronic equipment carried by modern warships and the complexities of a future war, one element remains as true today as it was in the time of the first Queen Elizabeth – the splendid character and calibre of the people who make up the Navy. This is a heritage which has to be maintained. The Royal Navy has had a glorious past, and those who serve will ensure that it has an equally glorious future.

INDEX

Printed in England for Her Majesty's Stationery Office by Staples Printers St Albans Limited at The Priory Press
Dd 696436 C50